TODAY'S TELLER
DEVELOPING BASIC SKILLS

Student Handbook

This publication is designed to provide accurate and authoritative information in regard to the subject matter covered. It is sold with the understanding that the publisher is not engaged in rendering legal, accounting, or other professional service. If legal advice or other expert assistance is required, the services of a competent professional person should be sought.

From a Declaration of Principles jointly adopted by a Committee of the American Bar Association and a Committee of Publishers and Associations.

The American Bankers Association is committed to providing innovative, high-quality products and services that are responsive to its members' critical needs.

To comment about this product, or to learn more about the American Bankers Association and the many products and services it offers, please call 1-800-BANKERS or visit our Web site: ***www.aba.com***.

This correspondence course has been approved by the American Bankers Association for use in courses for which ABA certificates or diplomas (formerly American Institute of Banking (AIB) certificates or diplomas) are granted.

American Bankers Association®

CONTENTS

EXHIBITS

Job Aids

INTRODUCTION

You are about to embark on a rewarding career with your bank. The role of a teller is an important one, because most business transactions that take place in the bank branch are through a teller. Which means that for those customers, *you are the bank*.

The *Today's Teller* course will provide you with the insight you need to grow from a new teller to an informed, professional teller. While we use the job title "teller" in the course, your bank may refer to the function as cashier, customer service representative, financial services representative, or may use another job title.

Like many industries today, the nature of banking is rapidly changing due to advances in technology and communications. The role of the teller is likewise changing as banks adapt to the changing needs and preferences of bank customers. What has not changed is the importance of the customer experience with you as you assist them with their financial needs.

1

THE CHANGING ROLE OF THE TELLER

OUTLINE

Section 1: The Business of Banking

Section 2: Today's Professional Teller

Section 3: Performance Standards

Section 4: The New Teller

OBJECTIVES

When you have completed this module, you will be able to

- Describe the general structure of a bank and the business of banking
- Describe four common work principles adopted by successful tellers
- Cite the attributes and performance standards expected of today's professional teller
- Recognize the common feelings and reactions of new tellers, and identify techniques to overcome them

INTRODUCTION

Before you can begin to learn specifics about the teller function, you must first learn how your performance and actions support your bank's goals. In *The Changing Role of the Teller*, you will learn about the business of banking and the principles that bank tellers follow. You will review your specific teller standards and responsibilities and your job description. This course concludes with an overview of actions to take for progressing from a new teller to an experienced, professional teller.

SECTION 1: THE BUSINESS OF BANKING

Banks differ from other businesses in many ways. The most critical difference lies in the product you deal with on a daily basis—money. Money is critical to the operation of households and businesses, and for most people it is a very personal matter.

A bank is an institution that offers safety and security to depositors, pays interest on some types of deposit accounts so that depositors' money can grow, lends out deposited funds for worthwhile purposes, charges interest or finance charges, and facilitates the transfer of funds from one party to another.

For example, Sharon deposits $5,000 into a savings account. The bank takes this money, along with deposits from other customers, and lends Felipe $25,000 to purchase a new car. Felipe repays the loan amount plus the finance charges. Finance charges are the cost of the credit. The bank pays Sharon interest on the balance maintained in her savings account. Exhibit 1-1 illustrates graphically this definition of a bank and depicts the interrelationships among depositors, borrowers, and the bank.

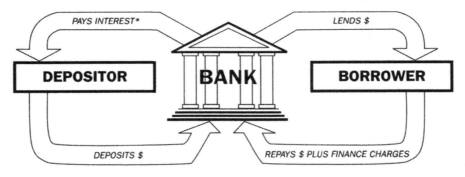

Exhibit 1-1   Bank's Relationship with Depositor and Borrower

How Do Banks Make Money?

Like all businesses, banks need to operate profitably to remain financially stable and secure in order to serve their customers effectively. Banks make money and earn profits in three ways. First, banks earn the majority of their profits through interest on loans. Second, banks earn interest by investing deposits. One type of investment is tax-exempt government bonds. And third, banks charge for services on checking accounts, savings accounts, and other bank products.

The Types of Financial Institutions

Banks are not the only institutions offering financial services. Today's consumers can have their financial needs met at a number of institutions. Exhibit 1-2 lists a few of the organizations that compete with banks or in some cases affiliate with them.

Exhibit 1-2 Types of Financial institutions and Services Offered

	Commercial banks	Savings and loans	Finance companies	Brokerage firms	Insurance companies
Insurance	●	●	●	●	●
Securities	●			●	●
Buy or rent real estate				●	●
Mortgages	●	●	●	●	●
Loans	●	●	●	●	●
Credit cards	●	●	●	●	●
Cash management	●	●	●	●	●
Money market	●	●	●	●	●
Pay interest	●	●	●	●	●
Check writing	●	●	●	●	●

Your vital role

How do you fit into the world of banking? What role does the teller position play in earning these profits and serving your customers? The successful teller plays a vital role in meeting the needs of the customer and achieving corporate goals. Next, you will review some principles that are basic to successful tellers in every bank.

SECTION 2: TODAY'S PROFESSIONAL TELLER

The Four Basic Teller Principles

Successful tellers have embraced certain common work principles. Adopting those principles will provide some basic guidelines you can use to meet your bank's expectations.

- The first principle is to **continually improve your customer service skills**. This enables you to provide excellent customer service
- The second principle is to **exercise great care when handling money and customer transactions**. This will ensure that your cash drawer balances at the end of the day. Keep in mind that although balancing is important, carefully handling transactions is also a customer service skill—preventing errors helps build the customer's trust in the bank
- Principle three is to **stay informed about the bank's products**. Product knowledge enables you to support the bank's sales goals and meet customers' needs
- And, the fourth principle is to **remain alert to possible security threats**. Be observant and fully informed about procedures for responding to possible security threats

Remembering these principles will be very beneficial as you learn more about the performance standards you are expected to meet.

SECTION 3: PERFORMANCE STANDARDS

Performance Expectations

When you are hired, you will receive a job description that outlines what is expected of you in your role as a teller. Your performance will be observed and reviewed on a regular basis. Although job descriptions may vary from bank to bank, banks commonly expect tellers to:

- **Show initiative** arising from a desire to excel and to contribute to the bank's goals
- **Be accurate**
- **Be consistent with bank policy**, following rules and policies communicated to you
- **Be efficient**—perform quickly and cost-effectively

To easily remember the four expectations, just think "I am an ACE!"

Initiative

Accurate

Consistent

Efficient

How expectations translate into performance standards

Performance expectations translate into the following eight specific performance standards.

Paying and receiving

You are expected to work accurately and efficiently when processing transactions. Throughout your day, you will give money to customers—who are making a withdrawal or cashing a check—and you will receive money from customers—to deposit in an account, purchase a negotiable item, or make a payment.

Performing related banking functions

You may also be expected to handle other banking services accurately and efficiently, such as handling safe deposit box rentals, exchanging foreign currency, or ordering checks.

Establishing and maintaining good customer relations

You are expected to establish and maintain good customer relations. This includes behaving professionally, friendly, and polite when assisting customers. You will be expected to keep existing customers and gain new customers for the bank through your behavior.

Recommending other bank products and services

You are expected to tactfully suggest specific bank products to customers who appear to need them. This is called cross-selling, and it involves telling the customer about the important features of the product, pointing out how the customer will benefit from using that product, and referring the customer to the bank representative who can provide more information.

Performing operations and balancing cash

You are expected to perform all bank procedures according to bank policy. Bank policy incorporates all federal and state legislation applicable to the performance of a given transaction.

In addition, you are expected to balance your cash drawer at the end of each working day (and possibly at other intervals). Essentially, this means you must account for all the cash you take in and all the cash you disburse.

Practicing sound loss-control procedures

You are expected to remain alert to all security conditions, both threatening and nonthreatening, that might cause bank losses. This means you will process transactions carefully, using the information you are learning now to avoid the loss problems that can plague tellers. In particular, you must understand and follow bank guidelines in robbery situations to protect your own safety and that of your customers and coworkers.

Assisting in other banking activities

You are expected to willingly perform many other duties as directed by your supervisor. Other duties may include cross-training for other bank positions, researching customer inquiries, taking over as head teller at lunchtime, or attending a training session.

Understanding banking laws and regulations

You are expected to be able to offer customers sound, sensible explanations for the various banking rules you must follow. This helps the customer understand why certain requirements exist and gives the customer confidence that you understand your job.

Rewards of a Job Well Done

Tellers who perform according to these expectations will experience the satisfaction of knowing they have done their jobs well. Tangible rewards (such as raises or bonuses) as well as increased customer satisfaction are also possible results of meeting these expectations.

In addition, you should continually be alert for ways to

- Improve your people skills
- Improve your organizational skills
- Maintain a positive attitude
- Maintain a professional appearance

If you demonstrate these attributes as you complete each teller performance standard, you are on your way to success. You will also discover the following Job Aid (1-1) to be an important resource when developing high-level teller skills.

JOB AID 1-1   HELPFUL HINTS FOR THE NEW TELLER

- Being organized is critical for success
    - Set up your cash drawer the same way each time
    - Have the right supplies on hand
    - Develop routines to help you stay organized and to alert you to possible fraudulent situations

- Communication basics
    - Put work aside and greet customers pleasantly
    - Make and maintain effective eye contact
    - Smile!
    - Use the customer's name
    - Listen actively
    - Rephrase an explanation to help the customer understand
    - Take notes
    - Avoid using acronyms
    - Close pleasantly

- Handling stress when customer lines form
    - Stay calm
    - Respond to the line of customers with positive eye contact and empathy
    - Be pleasant; apologize for any inconvenience; and thank customers for their patience
    - Get help if you need it
    - Stay positive

- Service is the key to success!
    - Put yourself in the shoes of your customers and treat them the way you would like to be treated in the same situation

EXERCISE 1-1 YOUR NEW CAREER

1. Working with your trainer, obtain a copy of your job description, responsibilities, and performance standards.
   a. Which area of your job looks the most interesting? Why?

   b. The least interesting? Why?

2. Review your teller training schedule with your trainer. Do you have concerns about a specific area of training? What are they?

3. Obtain a copy of your bank's missions and goals statement.
   a. What goal of your bank has the highest priority?

   b. How can you help the bank achieve those goals? Use your job description to answer this question.

When finished with the exercise, review your responses with your trainer or supervisor.

SECTION 4: THE NEW TELLER

Less experienced tellers are frequently overwhelmed by the amount of information they are expected to learn. Such feelings are normal in beginning a new career.

The five common new-teller reactions and what you can do to counteract them are as follows:

- Feeling overwhelmed
  - Focus on one thing at a time
  - Remember that everyone feels uncomfortable at first
  - Be patient with yourself

- Feeling slow and clumsy
  - Be realistic
  - Focus on accuracy
  - Be assured that most customers are understanding

- Feeling uncertain
  - Ask questions. That is part of the learning process
  - Do not wait to ask questions. Ask for help as soon as you need it
  - Remember—there is no such thing as a dumb question

- Experiencing information overload
  - Remind yourself that forgetting a few things is normal
  - Reassure yourself that the information will come back
  - Stay calm

- Feeling shunned by customers
  - It is human nature for people to react to change
  - Since you are new, you are the "change"

MODULE 1 REVIEW QUIZ

1. What are the four basic principles that all successful tellers adhere to?

2. What are the three primary ways a bank makes money?

3. Name at least four teller performance standards.

4. Name at least three common new teller reactions.

2

HANDLING CHECKS

OUTLINE

OBJECTIVES

When you have completed this module, you will be able to

- Identify the different components of a check
- Determine if a check is negotiable and acceptable
- Recognize warning signs that may indicate a forged or altered check
- Determine that each check has been endorsed appropriately
- Recognize acceptable forms of identification

INTRODUCTION

As a teller, you will spend most of your time handling transactions that involve checks. The purpose of a check is to transfer funds from one party to another.

In *Handling Checks*, you will learn about the different types of checks and how to determine if a check meets the requirements to be accepted for deposit or cashed. There are a variety of requirements, which involve the information on the front of the check and the words written or stamped on the back of the check.

This course will provide you with the foundational information needed to handle check transactions. Be sure to talk with your supervisor about your bank's specific policies and procedures.

SECTION 1: COMPONENTS OF A CHECK

It will be helpful to learn some common terms used to refer to specific components of a check. The common terms include payee/endorser, drawee, and maker. These are the three parties to a check.

Review the definitions below of each component.

- *Date:* The date on the check tells the bank when the maker intends to make the funds available to the payee.
- *Dollar amount:* Most checks show the dollar amount written out in **script format** and in **numeric format**.
- *Maker:* This is the person who wrote and signed the check, authorizing the bank to transfer funds to the payee. The maker may be one or more individuals acting on their own behalf or authorized to act on behalf of a business, organization, or governmental agency. The maker is also referred to as the check writer or drawer.
- *MICR encoding:* The term "magnetic ink character recognition" refers to the magnetic codes on the bottom of a check that allow a machine to read information specific to that check. Most MICR encoded lines include: the bank's routing number, the account number, and the serial number of the check.
- *Drawee:* Generally, the bank of the person writing the check. The drawee is also referred to as the check writer's bank.
- *Payee:* The recipient of the funds. The payee can be one or more individuals, a business, organization, government agency, cash, or bearer.
- *Transit number:* Also known as the routing number, routing transit number, and ABA number. This number identifies the bank where the account is located. The number appears as a fraction in the upper right corner of most checks as well as in the MICR encoding. Any checks that are missing the transit number in either of these locations should be referred to your supervisor. (See appendix B— Routing Transit Number: Federal Reserve Districts and Branch Cities.)

Exhibit 2-1   Components of a Check

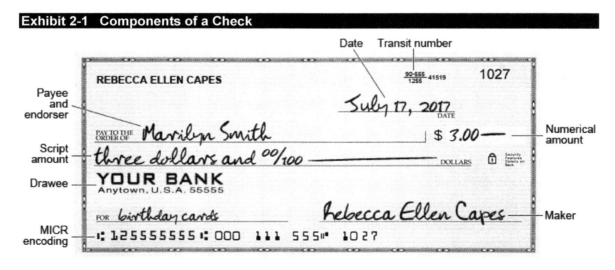

There is much to learn about checks. You are now familiar with some common terms used to identify the parts of a check. Review those parts to see if the item meets all the requirements for negotiability.

SECTION 2: NEGOTIABILITY

What is required to make a check a negotiable item?

A document that promises payment to a specific person(s) or entity(ies) is a negotiable item. The document must be easily transferable from one party to another by endorsement and delivery or delivery alone. For a check to be negotiable, it must meet certain requirements:

- The item must be **written**. A verbal commitment does not meet the requirements for being a negotiable item.
- The item must be **exchangeable for cash**. The payee must be able to receive cash when the item is presented to the bank.
- The item must have a **specific dollar amount**. There must be a specific dollar amount written on the document.
- The item must be **payable to a specific payee**. Payees can be companies, individuals, associations, nonprofit entities—whoever the maker of the check intends to pay. An item can also be made out to "cash" or "bearer." In the case of "cash" or "bearer," whoever possesses the item may negotiate it. Ask your supervisor if your bank accepts checks made payable to "bearer."
- The item must be **signed by the maker** of the check (check writer). Some checks produced through online banking providers say "Signature on File" instead of containing an actual signature. Consult your supervisor for guidance on how your bank handles such checks.
- The item should be **dated**. Although banks prefer to have a date on a check, it is not a legal requirement. Check with your supervisor to determine how to proceed if you receive a check without a date.
- The item must contain an **unconditional order to pay**. Look for words of negotiability, such as "Pay to the order of" or "Pay to." If these words are missing from an item presented to you by a customer, consult your supervisor before continuing the transaction.

SECTION 3: ACCEPTABILITY

In addition to being negotiable, a check must be acceptable. Criteria for check acceptance that are common to many banks include:

- **Checks may not be postdated or stale-dated.** Postdated means the check is dated in the future; stale-dated means the check is more than six months old. (Most banks state in their deposit account agreement that they will not honor checks over six months old. If a check is processed electronically through in-clearing, it may not be possible to identify the date; nevertheless, a good teller should always question a check over six months old)
- **The check must be signed by the maker exactly as the signature appears on the signature card or deposit agreement of the maker.** Electronically generated checks

(online banking) will have words to the effect of "signature on file" on the signature line. Your bank will have a policy about whether to cash such checks

- **There must be no indication that the check has been altered.** For example, the dollar amount and/or the name of the payee should not be altered
- **The maker's account must have sufficient funds to cover the amount of the check.** If the check is drawn on another bank-a transit check-then some banks require tellers to ascertain whether the payee's account has enough funds to cover the check
- **No stop payments can exist on an acceptable check.** A stop payment is an order to the bank by the maker of the check to refuse payment on the check. A person may wish to stop payment on a check or checks for several reasons: a checkbook was stolen, the payee never received the check, or the check was misplaced. For this service, the bank charges a fee. A stop payment order (SPO) is usually in effect for six months unless renewed by the account owner. The process for creating SPOs varies from bank to bank, so learn your bank's policy so that you can explain it to customers who ask
- **The person presenting the check should be your bank's customer, or the check must be drawn on your bank.** Check with your supervisor for your bank's policy If the check is not drawn on your bank, and if the presenter is not your bank's customer, consult with your supervisor before accepting the check

Important: Your bank is responsible for the negotiability and acceptability of every item you cash or deposit for customers. You must follow the policies and procedures of your bank very carefully.

SECTION 4: TYPES OF CHECKS

As a teller you will see several types of checks. The most common check types include:

- *Personal checks.* Personal checks are drawn on accounts owned by one or more individuals. Typically, personal checks are smaller than business checks and are easily identified by the individual's names in the upper left corner of the check (exhibit 2-1)
- *Business checks.* Business checks are drawn on accounts owned by businesses, corporations, and so forth. They are often larger in size than personal checks and have the name of the business printed in the upper left corner of the check. Business checks tend to be computer generated (exhibit 2-2)

Exhibit 2-2   Business Check

Big Time Business	7654
3333 Boulevard	22-2222/222
West Coast, CA 55555	

Date _____

Pay to the
order of _____ $ [   ]

_____ DOLLARS

YOUR BANK
Anytown, USA 55555
For _____   _____

7654   234000023⑆   000613502695 ⑈

- *Cashier's checks or official checks.* A cashier's check, also called an official check, is a check drawn by a bank on itself. There is no maximum issue amount for a cashier's check. However, tellers often have individual limits on the dollar amount they can issue without approval. Cashier's checks are used by customers who require guaranteed funds, such as for home closing costs or purchasing a car. Cashier's checks are also given to customers who are closing a bank account and want to deposit the funds at another financial institution (exhibit 2-3)

Exhibit 2-3   Cashier's Check

CASHIER'S CHECK

NO. 24305

August 14, 20 XX   12-345 / 678

PAY TO THE ORDER OF William T. Wrigley $ 150.00

150.00   DOLLARS

YOUR BANK
Your Town, Your State

SPECIMEN

Cashier

⑈024305⑈   ⑆0678⑈03457⑆   71⑈616 7⑈   ⑈0000015000⑈

- *Money orders.* A money order is a check drawn by a bank on itself or another bank. Money orders are also sold by the United States Postal Service, grocery stores, convenience stores, and companies such as Western Union® and MoneyGram®. They are used most often by customers who either do not have checking accounts or must have guaranteed funds (for example, to make a rent payment). A money order is most often negotiable, acceptable, and guaranteed by the bank to be good up to the amount specified on the money order. Ask your supervisor about your bank's procedure for handling money orders (exhibit 2-4)

Exhibit 2-4   Money Order

ABC BANK Money Order

Date _____   07-17435649

Pay the sum of _____110_____ dollars and __07__ cents
                              Not good over $500.

Pay to the order of _____

Sender's Name and Address _____

_____

Payable at ABC BANK, NY, NY   Josie Doe, Treasurer

⑃ 0711147 83 04   ⑈540717 35649⑈

- *Traveler's checks.* In the past, traveler's checks were frequently used by individuals traveling on vacation to foreign countries to purchase goods and services, and to exchange for local currency. However, with the increasing use of credit and debit cards, along with the availability of ATMs worldwide, traveler's checks are no longer common. These checks are sold in a variety of denominations. They are signed by the purchaser upon purchase and again, in the presence of the payee, when cashing the check to receive local currency or using it to pay for goods or services. Ask your supervisor about your bank's procedure for handling traveler's checks (exhibit 2-5)

Exhibit 2-5   Traveler's Check

- *Substitute checks.* A substitute check is a special paper copy of the front and back of an original check. The substitute check may be slightly larger than the original check. Substitute checks are specially formatted so they can be processed as if they were original checks. The front of a substitute check should state: "This is a legal copy of your check. You can use it the same way you would use the original check." **These checks can be accepted for deposit, but should never be cashed.** Check with your supervisor to learn about your bank's procedures for handling substitute checks at the teller line

- *Blank checks or counter checks.* Although this service is not as common today as it was in the past, some banks offer counter checks for customers who have forgotten their checkbooks or have run out of checks. These checks are encoded with the customer's account number. Bank policy on how these checks are issued will vary. Some banks have the encoding machines available in each office. Other banks must order the encoded checks from a central location (exhibit 2-6).

Exhibit 2-6   Counter Check

```
                                                      33-3333/333

                                    Date _____

Pay to the
order of _____  $ [_____]

_____ DOLLARS


YOUR BANK
Anytown, USA 55555
For _____        _____
```

- *Insurance Draft:* These negotiable instruments may be payable to one or more parties and are issued by insurance companies to pay insurance claims. Insurance drafts are not checks. The maker (insurance company) has the option to examine the item upon presentation at the drawee bank before deciding to pay or return the item. The words, "Payable Through" and the name of a bank will typically appear on the front of the draft. These drafts **should not be cashed** because they are subject to the insurance company "releasing" them or authorizing payment subject to certain provisions. Check with your supervisor before depositing these items into an account (exhibit 2-7).

Exhibit 2-7   Insurance Draft

```
┌─────────────────────────────────────────────────────────────┐
│  Safety Insurance Company            DRAFT NO. 222            │
│  44 Long View Drive                                           │
│  Commerce, VA 55555                                           │
│                                                               │
│                                  Date_____         │
│                                                               │
│  Pay to_____  $_____            │
│                                                               │
│  _____ DOLLARS          │
│                                                               │
│  Payable through                                              │
│  Your Bank                                                    │
│  Anytown, USA 55555                                          │
│                                                               │
│  _____         _____          │
└─────────────────────────────────────────────────────────────┘
```

- *Convenience Checks:* Convenience checks can be deposited into the maker's account. The checks may be used to transfer balances from one credit card company to another or for any other purpose. When the checks are used, the amount is added to a credit card balance of the maker (exhibit 2-8).

The credit card company may place restrictions on the amount available to the drawer and how the checks can be used. You should ask a supervisor for assistance if presented with one of these checks.

Exhibit 2-8   Convenience Check

```
┌──────────────────────────────────────────────────────────────┐
│ 5.99%  │  Harry Customer                           1356        │
│        │  1111 Anystreet                           999         │
│        │  Anywhere, MO 55555                       56-1661/441 │
│        │                          Date_____             │
│        │  Pay to the                                           │
│        │  order of_____  $_____        │
│  1356  │                                          DOLLARS      │
│        │  This document contains protection against alterations, a watermark and a microscopic signature line. Absence of these features will indicate a copy. │
│        │  Payable Through:            *Check void for all purposes after February 15, 2002. Must post │
│        │  First USA Management Services, Inc.   to your account by September 30, 2001 to get your 5.99% APR. │
│        │  Delaware, OH 43015                                   │
│        │  108                                                  │
│        │  Memo_____   Signature_____     │
│        │  ⑆044115511⑆370229224 10733⑈1356                      │
└──────────────────────────────────────────────────────────────┘
```

EXERCISE 2-1 NEGOTIATING CHECKS

Fill in the blanks with the correct answers.

1. A stale-dated check is more than _____ months old.
2. A postdated check is dated _____.
3. The amount on a check is written twice, once in _____ and once in _____.
4. The person who writes the check is called the _____.
5. On the following check, identify the (a) maker, (b) date, (c) payee, (d) drawee bank, and (e) amount. (f) Is this item negotiable? (Assume today's date is 12/15/17.)

   a. _____

   b. _____

   c. _____

   d. _____

   e. _____

   f. _____

MICHAEL L. WADE   1384

_____ 12-10 2017 1-8/210

PAY TO THE ORDER OF *Maria Valdez* $ 250 ⁵⁰/₁₀₀

two hundred fifty and ⁵⁰/₁₀₀ _____ DOLLARS

BIG BUX BANK
1235 Anystreet
Anytown, GA 55555

FOR _____   *Michael L. Wade*

⑆00000000 ⑆00000000000000⑈ 1384

SECTION 5: FORGED AND ALTERED DOCUMENTS

Forgery

What is forgery? Who commits it? Why do you have to be concerned about it, and what should you do if you encounter a forged document? The American Bankers Association defines check forgery as "the alteration of a document or instrument with intent to defraud." Forgery is intentional. Anyone who creates or alters a document for the purpose of committing fraud is engaging in forgery. Many times, checks are stolen for the purpose of committing fraud. When the thief gives a stolen check to a teller, the account may be legitimate and have a good balance, but the signature of the maker will be forged.

Characteristics of Forged Documents

The most frequently forged document is a check. Modern computer equipment and desktop publishing software, color copiers and printers, and the like enable criminals to create fake documents easily and accurately. These fakes look so real that even bank tellers may be fooled. Some are counterfeit money orders, some are phony cashier's checks, and others look like they're from legitimate business accounts. The companies whose names appear may be real, but someone has dummied up the checks without the companies' knowledge. To combat this technology, some businesses and banks are investing in specialized products, such as positive pay systems and systems that embed nonreproducible, invisible information on checks that can be read only by a decoder at the bank. Despite modern technology, however, some forgers still try to trick tellers the old way.

Here are some common signals to look for in detecting forgery:

- The document appears **altered**. An altered item is a real document that has been changed deliberately from its original form. Things to look for:
    - The letters or figures in the dollar amounts appear "squeezed" (the result of the thief's attempting to increase the dollar amount of a stolen, signed check by inserting additional words or numbers)
    - The type of font used to print the customer's name looks different from the font used to print other information on the check
    - The name of the maker or payee appears to have been altered. Example: The payee and address have been altered, and the font does not match the amount and date font
    - Erasures or faded background behind the maker and payee names
    - The amount of the check is inconsistent with the information on the "memo" line of the check (a check for $10,000 with a memo "house cleaning" would be suspicious)
- The document appears **counterfeit**. A counterfeit is a document created to look like a genuine check

- The background of a counterfeit check often has blotchy or inconsistent coloring
- The MICR numbers on the bottom of the check may appear shiny
- The **signature does not match** the one on the signature card or identification.
  - Forged signatures will often be done with felt pens to make it more difficult to match the writing style. In fact, if a felt pen has been used, many banks will ask the presenter to sign the document again with a pen offered by the bank employee
  - The style of the signature (space between letters, where the t's are crossed and the i's are dotted, and so forth) may vary significantly from the way it appears on the signature card or the identification being used to negotiate the check
  - A signature that does not fit on the signature line may indicate a forgery (because most people adapt the size of their signature to fit in the allotted space)
- The texture of the document **appears rough**, indicating erasures. When anyone tries to erase part of a check, the texture of the erased section becomes rough and the coloring on the check fades or disappears
- Look for **at least one perforated edge** on the check. The perforation shows that the check had been connected either to a checkbook or to other computer-printed checks. Counterfeit checks frequently do not have this perforated edge because they are printed on normal sheets of paper and cut apart. Exceptions to this are government and traveler's checks, which do not have a perforated edge
- Be alert for checks whose **color smears** when rubbed with a moist finger. This suggests they were prepared on a color copier to give the appearance of a colored check

Detecting Altered Checks

Criminals are always finding ways to swindle the public. For example, checks are often stolen out of the mail, altered, and then presented to a teller to get cash. To prevent your bank from suffering a loss, always compare the figure amount with the written amount. Watch for squeezed-in numbers or different colors of ink. Look for erasures, different writing styles, and the use of felt tip markers.

One type of alteration is changing a company name to a personal name, such as "Marilyn & Co." to "Marilyn H. Combs." In this example, the "&" might have been erased and the "H" inserted to fill in the space. Other alterations can be as simple as changing "I.R.S." to "I.R.Smythe."

Get in the habit of examining the date, the numerical amount, the written amount, the maker's signature, the maker's bank name, and the payee name.

Procedures for Handling Forged or Altered Documents

Follow your bank's procedures if you suspect a check is forged or has been altered. In general, these are the five check verifications to make

1. Verify the account name matches the maker's signature
2. Attempt to contact the maker to confirm the payee and dollar amount
3. If in doubt about the endorsement, have the customer re-endorse the document in your presence
4. Ensure that you have acceptable identification and that the identification is genuine
5. Consult your supervisor if you have any doubt about any item presented at your teller window

You must take advance precautions against forgery. Keep telephone numbers for security personnel handy in case you need another opinion or have a question. Keep verification sources and security checklists nearby and up to date.

Some banks ask noncustomers to provide a fingerprint on the check using a special clear ink. The fingerprint is placed between the memo line and the signature line on the check being cashed. If the check is returned, law enforcement officials are given the check with the fingerprint of the individual who cashed it.

Who Commits Forgery?

Do not rely on your instincts to identify forgers. Appearance is no predictor of honesty. Anyone can be a forger. Persons of all ages, races, and professions commit forgery. Inexperienced forgers anxious about being caught in fraud may seem exceptionally nervous or rushed. However, those who have successfully forged documents in the past may not offer such obvious clues to what they are attempting to do. Looking honest is no guarantee of honesty. The best defense against forgery is to follow your bank's verification procedures.

Although approximately 70 percent of forgery activity occurs from October to December, you should be constantly aware of the possibility that the item you are receiving at your teller window could be forged or altered. Once again, the best defense against attempts at forgery is to follow your bank's procedures.

Acting on Forgeries

What should you do when you suspect a forgery?
- Follow bank policy
- Be discreet; do not make a scene; *never accuse a suspect*
- Politely excuse yourself from the window while you compare the customer's signature card (if available) and identification with what is on the check being presented
- Check with your supervisor if your analysis of the handwriting causes you to doubt the signature or if the item itself appears to be a forgery
- *Do not give out money if you suspect forgery. Get help!*

EXERCISE 2-2 POTENTIAL FORGERS

Review your bank's procedures on handling suspected forgeries. Then complete this exercise.

You work for a large, regional bank. A professionally dressed man, who is not a bank customer, approaches your window and requests that you cash the check below. The check is drawn on an account with your bank.

1. Should you cash the check?

2. What details about the check would cause you to suspect a forgery?

3. How should you handle the suspected forgery?

EXERCISE 2-3 FORGERY

1. What is forgery?

2. Who commits forgery?

3. List four signals that should make you suspect a document has been forged.

4. List five things you should do if you suspect forgery.

5. How might a check payable to "Harrison & Co." be altered?

6. If you are presented a check with different colors of ink and different writing styles, what should you do at your bank?

SECTION 6: ENDORSEMENTS

Principles of Endorsements

Many factors determine if a check can be accepted for deposit or cashed. One of those factors is having a correct endorsement. Every check that is presented with a deposit slip or to be cashed must be endorsed. An endorsement is the signature or stamp placed on the back of the check. The signature or stamp is what allows ownership of the funds to be transferred from the writer of the check to the payee. Whoever endorses the check also assumes responsibility for the amount of the check if it is returned by the check writer's bank. For example, if Jack Smith deposits a check from Linda Jones and the check is returned by Linda's bank, Jack's account will be charged for the check amount.

Here are some basic rules for endorsing checks:

- *All endorsements should be in ink.* Pencil endorsements fade easily and are difficult to read on returned items and copies. Felt tip pens are discouraged because they are often used by forgers who rely on the thick lines to conceal handwriting differences. Most banks will ask the customer to re-endorse the check if the endorsement has been done in pencil or felt tip pen

- *Checks should be endorsed in your presence, if in doubt.* You will find that many customers will already have endorsed the checks before presenting them to you. If you do not know the customer or have any doubt about the endorsement, ask the customer to re-endorse the check in your presence

- *The check must be endorsed exactly as the name appears on the payee line of the check.* For example, your customer Sharon brings in a check she wants to deposit. The check is made payable to *Sharon T. Jones*. Sharon has endorsed the check with *S. Jones*. Even though Sharon signed her signature card as S. Jones, you will need to ask her to re-endorse the check as *Sharon T. Jones*—exactly as it is written in the payee line

  – What if the maker of the check has spelled your customer's name incorrectly? For example, *Mike Whyte* has received a check made payable to *Mike White*. In this situation, you will ask Mike to endorse the check exactly as it appears on the payee line, then re-endorse it with the correct spelling. On the back of the check Mike will need to endorse first as *Mike White*, then again as *Mike Whyte*

- *A check made payable to joint payees with the designation "and" must contain the endorsements of all payees.* For example, a check made payable to *Joe Garcia and Marge Garcia* must be endorsed separately by Joe and Marge.

- *When the designation "or" is used for alternate payees, only one endorsement is necessary.* For example, a check made payable to *Joe Garcia or Marge Garcia* can be endorsed by either Joe or Marge. It is not necessary for both of them to endorse the check. Also, a check payable to *Joe Garcia, Marge Garcia* (without an "or") is presumed to be "or" and either person may endorse the check.

Important: When presented with checks made payable to more than two payees, check with your supervisor before you complete the transaction.

Endorsement Types

There are three common endorsement types: general (blank), restrictive, and stamped endorsements. Less common are special and conditional endorsements.

A **general** or **blank** endorsement is the most common endorsement you will see. This endorsement shows only the names of the payee(s). It is considered "blank" because there are no additional instructions or limitations; the check can be deposited or cashed.

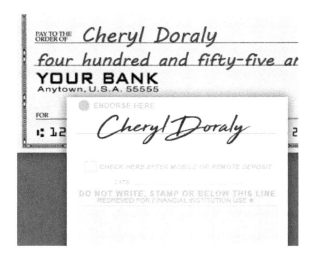

A check may have a single payee or multiple payees. When there is only one payee named on a check, that one person alone has the right and responsibility to endorse the check. However, when multiple payees are listed, ownership of the funds depends on how the maker wrote the check. If the names are connected by the word "AND," all payees must endorse the check (joint payees). If the names are connected by the word "OR," then only one of the payees must sign (alternate payees).

A **restrictive** endorsement imposes limitations on what can be done with the check. In this example, the restriction states the check is only to be deposited in the endorser's account, not cashed.

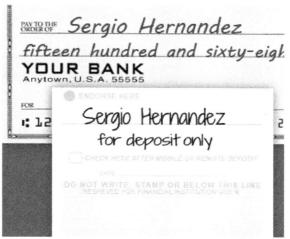

A **stamped** endorsement is made with a rubber stamp, often by businesses. Checks bearing a stamped endorsement must be deposited into an account with the same name as the endorsement. In this example, the check must be deposited into an account that has been opened under the name "Bill's Pool Service." A check made payable to a business must be deposited into an account in the name of that business. The check cannot be deposited into the personal account of the owner and the check cannot be cashed.

A **special** endorsement is used by the payee to legally give the check to someone else. For example, if Lucius Friday owes Maria Smith $50, and he is the payee on a check for $50, rather than cash the check, he can use the special endorsement to sign the check over to Maria. Lucius would write "Pay to the order of Maria Smith" on the back of the check and then sign it. Maria would also need to endorse the check (sign it) in order to deposit the check or cash it. You must be able to identify both endorsers' signatures. Due to the risks involved with a special endorsement, consult with your supervisor before accepting these checks for deposit or cashing these checks.

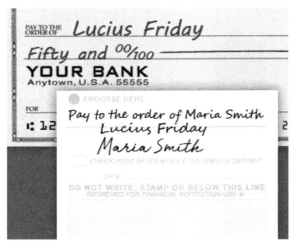

A **conditional** endorsement imposes on the bank the responsibility of determining whether the condition included in the endorsement has been fulfilled. In this example, the bank has no way of knowing if the garage work has been completed. Most banks do not accept a conditional endorsement. If a bank does accept this endorsement, it normally requires a supervisor's approval to cash. Typically, the supervisor will not approve this check unless the conditions are removed.

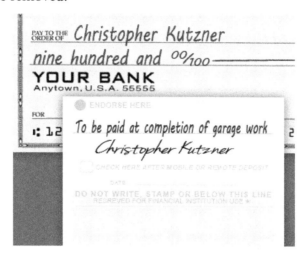

EXERCISE 2-4 TYPES OF ENDORSEMENTS

What form of endorsement is represented on the back of each of these checks? Should you negotiate the item (either for cash or deposit)?

1. Pay to the order of
   Harold Johnston
   Marilyn Carter

2. Walter Cross

3. For Deposit Only
   Laura Kutzning

4. Payable upon college graduation
   Jed Barnowski

5. **Johnson Dog Food**

Below each check write the proper endorsement for each check and name the type of endorsement.

6.

Ruben & Ellen Finestein		1234
Old Town Road		
Goodplace, Ohio 55555	9-4 20 XX	1-8 / 210

PAY TO THE ORDER OF *John and Marlissa Jones* $ *10.00* —

Jen _____ DOLLARS

YOUR BANK

MEMO *anniversary* *Ruben Finestein*

⑆021000089⑈ 584557881⑈

7.

Terence J. Cartwright		124
050 Some Street		
Dream Town, BB 66556	3-5 20 XX	1-8 / 210

PAY TO THE ORDER OF *Internal Revenue Service* $ *374.32*

Three hundred seventy four 32/100 _____ DOLLARS

YOUR BANK

MEMO *20XX taxes* *Terence J. Cartwright*

⑆021000089⑈ 584557881⑈

8.

Robert Adams		787
50 Phosphate Drive		
Fireville, GA 21212	5-16 20 XX	1-8 / 210

PAY TO THE ORDER OF *Cash* $ *100.00* —

One hundred _____ DOLLARS

YOUR BANK

MEMO *misc.* *Robert Adams*

⑆021000089⑈ 584557881⑈

SECTION 7: IDENTIFICATION AND SIGNATURES

Identification

"Until I know you better, may I see some identification please?" As a teller, this is one question you cannot escape asking. But be warned—even though this question is asked routinely of bank customers, some customers will respond emotionally to it because they see it as a challenge to their integrity. You may be able to rephrase the question to make it seem less challenging, but you cannot escape asking for ID from many of your customers every day.

Why all the fuss about identification?

Consider the following scenario: Your wallet is stolen, and it contains your monthly paycheck, considerable cash, your driver's license, your bank ID card, and your credit cards.

Whoever stole your wallet will probably try to cash your check. The thief has enough information from your wallet to forge your signature and cash your paycheck, and even to produce a second form of ID, such as your bank ID or a credit card.

If a thief tried to cash *your* paycheck, what kind of security would you have? This answer is, a teller, specifically, a teller who follows bank policy on asking for and recording information from the ID before cashing the check. Such a teller would notice that the photo on the driver's license does not resemble the person cashing the check or that the ID had been altered.

Whenever you are giving a customer something—cash, a cashier's check, information about an account, etc.—you will be required to positively identify the customer at your window.

Verifying every customer's identification prevents you from giving a customer's money or account information to an unauthorized person.

When you accept an endorser's identification, enter the identification details directly into your bank's transaction system by keying it on the computer. This information can be used to track the payee if the check is returned for any reason. You will be held accountable for all decisions you make to accept identification.

Take the time to examine identification carefully. Remember, each time you ask for identification, you are protecting your customer's account. It is difficult to explain to a valued customer that you gave away money from his or her account simply because you ignored procedure and failed to ask for identification.

Forged Endorsements

Forgers intentionally come to the bank or the drive-in window during the busy time from 11:00 a.m. to 1:00 p.m. or near closing, but they may come at any time. They know that when you are rushing to help lunch-hour customers or are focusing on closing activities your attention may be diverted more easily from their transaction. Diverting your attention is how forgers succeed.

Use the following guidelines when examining endorsements:

- Closely examine each check and each presenter
- Do not be afraid to ask for identification
- Never let the presenter hurry your examination of the check or the identification
- Ensure that the
    - Endorsement matches the signature on their ID
    - ID belongs to the person at your window
    - ID is genuine

The most common identification is a driver's license with a photograph. It has such information as age, height, weight, and signature and a photograph that will help you decide whether an endorsement is valid. Always examine identification carefully for alterations. The identification should convince you that the appropriate individual is presenting the transaction.

Acceptable Forms of Identification

You will be shown many types of identification from customers who want to cash checks. *Not all credentials are acceptable identification.*

Various forms of identification are described below, along with some common instructions about what to record.

- **Valid driver's license.** Record expiration date, payee's birth date, and driver's license number.
- **Valid in-state identification card.** Record expiration date, payee's birth date, and identification number.
- **Alien Registration Card (Green Card) or Matricula Consular Card.** Ask your supervisor if your bank accepts these as a valid form of primary identification.
- **Valid passport.** Record expiration date, passport number, and issuing country.
- **Current military photo ID.** Record expiration date, birth date, number, and name of the division of the military.
- **Recognition by a bank employee you know.** Have the employee you know, who identifies your customer, initial the check, assuming full responsibility.

Note: Your bank's instructions may differ. Check with your supervisor to see what notations your bank requires for each form of ID.

Unacceptable Forms of Identification

The following substitutes for identification generally are not acceptable:

- The customer makes a verbal reference to being acquainted with a reputable person, such as a notable community figure

- The customer appears to know a regular, well-known customer. You may see the unknown customer talking to your well-known customer. This is a common setup used by con artists. The con hopes that your observance of his "acquaintance" with the well-known customer will cause you to lower your guard and not ask to see identification or not look as closely at the identification when he asks you to cash a check
- The customer has an honest, conservative appearance. Appearance is no indicator of honesty or wealth
- The customer presents identification that can be easily altered or forged, such as a library card, blood donor card, social security card, birth certificate, club membership, welfare ID, charitable organization card, or prison release card
- The customer presents valid, but expired, identification
- The customer's signature on the ID does not match the signature on the check presented for cashing

Note: Refer to your bank's specific identification guidelines.

Altered Identification

Learn to recognize these three common signs of altered identification cards:

1. The description alongside the picture does not match the person presenting the identification, even though the picture may match the customer
2. The picture or signature appears raised, smeared, or tampered with
3. One line or section of print may look different than the rest of the printing on the ID

Signatures

Detecting forged signatures can be difficult and time consuming. Some large banks use computer-based equipment to selectively analyze signatures, especially on large checks. The volume of checks is too large to make it practical to review the signatures of each one. Nevertheless, a teller can play an important role in detecting forged signatures.

Someone who keeps stolen identification for a while has time to practice making the signature that appears on it. Even so, few people are fully able to imitate another person's signature. If you look for the following warning signs, you will be less likely to miss a forged signature.

- The signature appears different from that on the signature card. Look at the slant and size of letters, dots over i's, the crossing of t's, curlicues, pressure, and comparative length of the entire signature
- The signature presented is illegible
- The strokes seem hesitant
- More than one pen has been used
- Letters appear written with uneven pressure
- The signature appears traced
- The signature appears shaky

Caution: Valid signatures of people who are elderly or ill may have some of the characteristics listed on the previous page. If you did not witness the customer's signature and you doubt its authenticity, politely explain that there appears to be a small discrepancy between the signature card and the signature on the check or withdrawal slip. Tell the customer that to protect his or her account, you must ask for another signature on a piece of paper. This request should verify the validity of your endorser, since a forgery is difficult to recreate quickly.

Some banks prefer to have a supervisor handle any questionable signatures. Check with your supervisor to see how you should handle these situations.

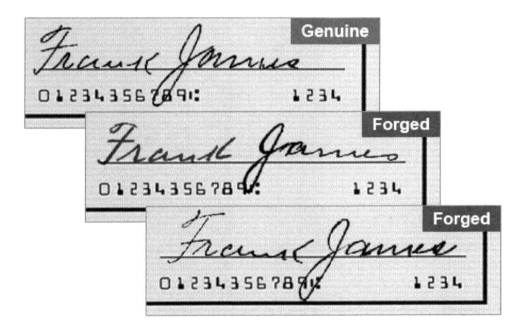

In summary, use the following steps for identification:

1. Ask to see the proper identification documents
2. Check the authenticity of the documents
3. Compare the photograph and the description on the document with the endorser
4. Examine the endorser's signature for signs of forgery and for similarity to the signature in the bank's file or on the identification document

EXERCISE 2-5 PROPER IDENTIFICATION

Review your bank's specific requirements, then place a Y (yes) next to identification you would accept and an N (no) next to identification you would not accept.

_____ valid passport

_____ library card

_____ social security card

_____ charitable organization card

_____ customer's apparent acquaintance with a well-known customer

_____ club membership card

_____ prison release card

_____ local blood donor card

_____ recognition by a bank officer or employee you know

_____ birth certificate

_____ current driver's license

_____ welfare ID

_____ current military ID with photo

_____ calling another employee by first name

JOB AID 2-1   CHECK-CASHING GUIDELINES

Review your bank's check-cashing guidelines, then answer the following questions. Keep this job aid handy for reference.

1. What is your check-cashing dollar limit for checks on your own bank?

2. What is your check-cashing dollar limit for checks on other banks?

3. Is the limit different for drive-in transactions?

4. How many pieces of identification are required for cashing checks?

5. Do you cash checks drawn on other banks for noncustomers? If so, list which of these transit checks you cash for noncustomers.

6. What questions do you have about your bank's check-cashing guidelines?

Hint: Place a copy of your bank's check-cashing guidelines in a convenient area of your window for easy reference.

EXERCISE 2-6   WOULD YOU CASH THIS CHECK?

Assume today's date is June 1, 2017. Follow your bank's teller limits. For each of the following checks answer these questions:

a. Is it negotiable? If not, why?

b. Would you cash it?

c. What will you tell the customer?

Hint: Negotiable means that the check includes the required items for negotiability. These requirements include words of negotiability ("Pay to the order of"), payable to a specific payee, written for a specific amount (the amount must be written twice—numbers and words), and signed by the maker (check writer).

1.
    a.
    b.
    c.

2.
    a.
    b.
    c.

Horatio and Darlene Lees
206 Almond St.
Candy Town, MN 02030   5-28   20 17   1-8/210

1602

PAY TO THE ORDER OF   *Cash* $33.00

Thirtee three   DOLLARS

YOUR BANK

MEMO _____   *Horatio Lees*

⑆021000089⑆   58455788⑈

3.

    a.

    b.

    c.

Carolyn Jacobson
200 Brook Lane
Silver Creek, CO 55455   4-15   20 17   1-8/210

107

PAY TO THE ORDER OF   *J. R. Smith* $345.00

Three hundred forty five   DOLLARS

YOUR BANK

MEMO *taxes*   *Carolyn Jacobson*

⑆021000089⑆   58455788⑈

4.

    a.

    b.

    c.

Jo Ann & John Busby
15 Acre Farm
Midland, TX 22112   6-4   20 17   1-8/210

426

PAY TO THE ORDER OF   *Marion Caywood* $20.00

Twenty   DOLLARS

YOUR BANK

MEMO *Carpool*   *Jo Ann Busby*

⑆021000089⑆   58455788⑈

5.

    a.

    b.

    c.

Minnie Bender
166 Highland Hills
Countryside, MA 11221

352

5-25   20 17   1-8/210

PAY TO THE ORDER OF *Lin Su Wong* $ 120.00 —

One hundred twenty ——————————— DOLLARS

YOUR BANK

MEMO _____   *Minnie Bender*

⑆021000089⑆   584557 88⑈

6.

   a.

   b.

   c.

Laraina Ashmore
050 Tree Street
Arborville, NM 85851

49

9-20   20 17   1-8/210

PAY TO THE ORDER OF *Jenelle Ashmore* $ 117.45 —

——————————————————— DOLLARS

YOUR BANK

MEMO *food*   *Laraina Ashmore*

⑆021000089⑆   584557 88⑈

7.

   a.

   b.

   c.

George S. George
55 Phoenix Place
Mythland, SD 29282

785

5-1   20 17   1-8/210

PAY TO THE ORDER OF *Scottie Johanson* $ 214.56 —

Two hundred fourteen 56/100 —————— DOLLARS

YOUR BANK

MEMO _____   _____

⑆021000089⑆   584557 88⑈

8.

   a.

   b.

   c.

MODULE 2 REVIEW QUIZ

1. What is a check?

2. Who are the three parties to a check?

   -
   -
   -

3. What seven characteristics make a check negotiable?

   -
   -
   -
   -
   -
   -
   -

4. What are the six common criteria for check acceptability?

   -
   -
   -
   -
   -
   -

5. For each condition below, indicate whether the check appears to be acceptable (A) or unacceptable (U) according to that single condition, without knowing anything else about the check.

   ____ Seven months old

   ____ Payable to an individual

   ____ Signed by the maker

   ____ A stop payment order is in effect from the maker

   ____ Insufficient funds exist in the maker's account

   ____ Dated tomorrow

6. What are three common signs of altered identification?

   •

   •

   •

7. Which of the following endorsements is used by the payee to legally give the check to someone else?

   ___ General or blank

   ___ Restrictive

   ___ Stamped

   ___ Special

   ___ Conditional

8. What five check verifications should be made when you suspect forgery?

   •

   •

   •

   •

   •

9. Which among the following are unacceptable identification sources?

   ___ Birth certificate

   ___ Driver's license

   ___ Alien Registration Card

   ___ Social Security card

   ___ Frequent flyer club card

   ___ Passport

10. If your identification and paycheck were stolen and the thief showed a teller your ID in an attempt to cash your paycheck, what would you hope the teller would do?

ANSWERS TO EXERCISES

Exercise 2-1: Negotiating Checks

1. 6 months
2. In the future
3. figures, words
4. Maker
5. a. Michael L. Wade
   b. 12/10/2017
   c. Maria Valdez
   d. Big Bux Bank
   e. $250.00
   f. Yes

Exercise 2-2: Potential Forgers

1. No; there are indications that the check is a forgery
2. Suspicious details:
   - The amount appears to be altered: The letters or figures in the dollar amounts appear "squeezed" (the result of the thief's attempting to increase the dollar amount of a stolen, signed check by inserting additional words or numbers)
   - The payee appears to be altered: erasures or faded background behind the payee names
   - The amount of the check is inconsistent with the information on the "memo" line of the check (the memo says "tree trimming" and the check amount is $19,000)
3. How you should handle the suspected forgery:
   - Follow bank policy
   - Be discreet; do not make a scene; never accuse a suspect
   - Check the signature card or identification
   - Politely excuse yourself from the window and check with your supervisor
   - Do not give out money if you suspect forgery. Get help!

Exercise 2-3: Forgery

1. Forgery is the creation or alteration of a document or instrument with fraudulent intent
2. People of all ages, races, and professions commit forgery
3. (1) The document appears altered. (2) The document appears counterfeit. (3) The document appears to have a forged signature. (4) The texture of the document appears rough

4. (1) Follow bank policy. (2) Be discreet. (3) Check the signature card or identification. (4) Check with the supervisor if the document indicates forgery. (5) Do not give out the money if you suspect a forgery
5. It might be altered to "Harrison H. Cofield." (Answers may vary)
6. Follow bank policy; do not negotiate the item without approval from a manager

Exercise 2-4: Types of Endorsements

1. Special. No, only if Harold Johnston is a well-known customer
2. Blank. Yes, unless you have some reason to suspect that the signature has been forged
3. Restrictive. Yes (deposit only)
4. Conditional. No, requires manager approval
5. Stamped. Yes
6. John Jones, Marlissa Jones. General (blank)
7. Stamped Internal Revenue Service. General (blank)
8. Generally, Robert Adams or whoever presents the check. General (blank)

Exercise 2-5: Proper Identification

Answers may vary by bank

  Y   valid passport

  N   library card

  N   social security card

  N   charitable organization card

  N   customer's apparent acquaintance with a well-known customer

  N   club membership card

  N   prison release card

  N   local blood donor card

  Y   recognition by a bank officer you know identifies customer

  N   birth certificate

  Y   current driver's license

  N   welfare ID

  Y   current military ID with photo

  N   calling another employee by first name

Exercise 2-6: Would You Cash This Check?

1. a. Yes
   b. No. The amounts do not agree
   c. Ask customer whether Mr. Parker can issue a new check
2. a. No. Missing words of negotiability
   b. No. In addition to being non-negotiable, the check is payable to a business and therefore must be deposited into the business account
   c. Because the check is payable to a business, it must be deposited into the business account
3. a. Yes
   b. No. Amounts have been altered
   c. Refer to manager
4. a. Yes
   b. No. Payee has been altered
   c. Refer to manager
5. a. Yes.
   b. No. Check is postdated
   c. Ask customer to return on 6/4/17
6. a. Yes
   b. Yes
   c. Not applicable
7. a. Yes
   b. No. The written amount is missing
   c. Refer to manager, and advise the customer that the check is incomplete
8. a. No. Maker's signature is missing.
   b. No.
   c. Ask customer to take the check to the maker for signature

3

PROCESSING TRANSACTIONS

OUTLINE

Section 1: Deposits

Section 2: Withdrawals and Cashing Checks

Section 3: Transaction Workflow

Section 4: Check 21

Section 5: Negotiable Instruments

Section 6: Loan Payments, Bankcard Transactions, and Foreign Currency

Section 7: Processing Large Cash Transactions

Section 8: Security When Processing Transactions

OBJECTIVES

When you have completed this module, you will be able to

- Process basic deposit and withdrawal transactions
- Describe the transaction workflow
- Identify substitute check requirements under Check 21
- Describe guidelines for handling negotiable instrument transactions
- Process basic loan payments, bankcard transactions, and foreign currency exchange
- Recognize transactions that require completing a Currency Transaction Report or Suspicious Activity Report
- Identify potential deposit fraud, check kiting transactions, and fraudulent cashier's checks

INTRODUCTION

As a teller, you will spend most of your work day processing transactions. The steps you take in these transactions are vitally important to the bank and your career.

When you follow bank policy and stay alert while processing each transaction, you are the first line of defense against forgery, attempted fraud, and check alterations.

You are also the face of the bank for each customer you serve. Remember these essential points while you process any customer transaction:

Always provide excellent customer service. The customer at your window is important. Although you may find yourself heavily involved in some complex procedures of a particular transaction, do not forget the polite and attentive behavior that helps provide the high-quality service your customer deserves.

Always follow your bank's procedures, and follow those procedures precisely. Unless authorized by your supervisor, do not skip any steps or modify policies. Remember security and loss prevention, product knowledge, sales, and courtesy is important at every step of every transaction.

Always pay attention. Preventing potential bank losses is an ongoing responsibility for every bank employee, but particularly for tellers. Tellers are the "collection point" for most of the checks presented by customers at your bank. Your knowledge and expertise in recognizing negotiable items and processing those items correctly is a key defense against bank losses.

In *Processing Transactions*, you will review the most common transactions related to deposits, withdrawals, negotiable items, loan payments, bankcard transactions, and foreign currency. You will also learn about regulations and security measures that affect your processing procedures.

The procedures in place at your bank are designed to ensure that regulations and security measures are followed to protect you, your bank, and your customers.

SECTION I: DEPOSITS

Deposits into Checking or Savings Accounts

The process for making a deposit into a checking or savings account varies from bank to bank. Customers can deposit cash and/or checks.

Customers might use preprinted checking account deposit slips or blank checking or savings deposit tickets to make their deposit. Some banks have systems in place that eliminate the need for deposit slips.

A properly completed deposit slip has the following information:

- Date, customer's name, and account number
- Total cash to be deposited
- A list of the checks being deposited
- The total amount (cash plus checks) being deposited
- Total cash to be returned to the customer as "less cash"

General guidelines when processing deposits.

- Ensure that the items listed on the deposit slip represent the actual items presented. Clear up any discrepancies before processing the deposit

- If currency and coin are being deposited, carefully count and verify the cash you receive against the amount on the deposit slip
- If checks are involved, examine each check for negotiability, acceptability, and proper endorsements
- Place the checks, the cash-in ticket (if applicable), and the deposit slip in your work tray or bin. Hand the receipt for the deposit to the customer
- If the customer is requesting cash back from the deposit, ask for identification
- Thank the customer for banking with your bank, and give him or her the receipt and any cash requested

Some banks process commercial deposits or deposits made by a third party to another customer's account differently so that the balance does not appear on the deposit receipt. Ask if your bank adheres to this policy.

Deposit Advice

Some businesses pay their employees by depositing their pay directly into bank accounts. The employees are given a "deposit advice" which is a confirmation of the deposit. Because these deposit advice notices look very similar to the check itself, many tellers have taken them as a deposit or even cashed them for customers.

The deposit advice will contain such words as "non-negotiable" or "This is not a check." If you see these words on an item being presented for deposit or to be cashed, politely explain to the customer that the item is not a check and offer to look into his or her account records to see if the amount showing on the deposit advice notice has in fact been deposited to his or her account (exhibit 3-1).

Exhibit 3-1   Deposit Advice

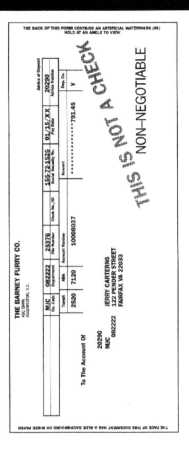

Credits and Debits

A big part of your job will be to ensure that the credits and debits you receive for each transaction are balanced.

Understanding credits and debits can be challenging as you begin learning how to process transactions. This will get you started: deposit slips and cash-out (cash given out) are always credits. Checks and cash-in (cash taken in) are always debits.

Examples of typical transactions you will see as a teller:

Mr. Jenkins is depositing his $253.00 expense check (a debit). He hands you his check and a deposit ticket (a credit) for $253.00. The debit and the credit in this transaction balance because they are both for the same amount.

Mrs. Baskin brings in two checks. One is for $125.00 and the other is for $50.00. She hands you a deposit ticket in the amount of $175.00. Does this transaction balance? The answer is yes. There are two debits (the checks for $125.00 and $50.00) that when added together total $175.00—the same amount as the credit (deposit ticket).

Working with debits and credits has frustrated many new tellers. Do not hesitate to ask someone for help as you learn how to work with these transactions.

Availability of Funds: Regulation CC

Sometimes banks place a hold on the funds from a check to restrict the customer from accessing the deposited funds right away. When a check drawn on another bank is presented to you, there is no way for you to know that the funds in the account will be there when the check reaches the drawee bank (check writer's bank). Therefore, you may be required to postpone the customer's access to the funds by placing a hold on the account for the amount of the check. The hold provides time for the check to reach the check writer's bank and for that bank to notify your bank whether or not they will honor the check and send the funds to your bank.

This hold is a protection for the bank and the customer against losses that could be incurred if the check is not honored and is returned unpaid to your bank.

The lengths of the holds on checking accounts are regulated by the Expedited Funds Availability Act (EFAA) of 1987, which is implemented by the Federal Reserve's Regulation CC.

Regulation CC Provisions

Each bank will have its own funds availability policy—based, of course, on Regulation CC's requirements—and all tellers in a bank must be able to explain the major provisions of their bank's policy. The following information highlights the major provisions of Regulation CC:

- Establishes maximum hold periods on checks
- Requires disclosures to customers of bank's hold policies
- Gives the Federal Reserve Board authority to improve the check collection and return system

Note: Your supervisor will give you some very specific procedures about how Regulation CC holds are handled at your bank.

Some specific provisions of Regulation CC most applicable to the teller position include the following requirements.

Banks must

- Make funds from a check available to the customer within a reasonable time
- Guarantee next-day availability to customers on deposits of less risky items, including:
  - Federal, state, and local government checks

- Cashier's checks
- Postal money orders
- Electronic funds transfers
- On-us checks
- Cash

Endorsement Requirements of Regulation CC

As a part of the effort to decrease the time it takes for checks to clear the drawee bank, Regulation CC also included some very specific guidelines about the placement of endorsements on checks (exhibit 3-2).

At least three endorsements appear on the back of every check: the payee, the depositary bank, and the collecting and returning bank.

The payee endorsement is confined to the 1½ inch area at the "trailing edge" of the check. This area is indicated on the back of checks.

The depositary bank is confined to the next 1½ inch area below the payee endorsement area. This is 3 inches from the leading edge of the check to 1½ inches from the trailing edge. The depositary bank's endorsement must be in purple or black ink.

Exhibit 3-2   Endorsement Standards

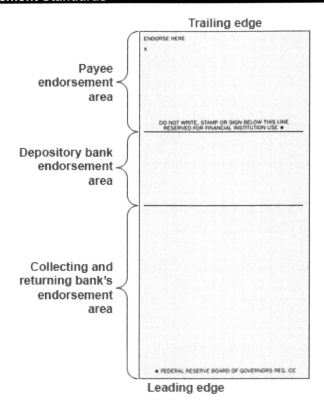

Caution: Some very costly penalties are involved with holds that have been handled incorrectly. Until you have gained considerable experience with Regulation CC holds, be sure to ask for help when placing holds and before answering customer questions.

EXERCISE 3-1   REGULATION CC

1. Name the three major provisions of Regulation CC.

2. Where should customers wishing to cash a check endorse the item?

3. Referring to your bank's brochure, describe as you would to a customer your bank's funds availability regulations.

JOB AID 3-1 REGULATION CC

To ensure that you understand how Regulation CC holds are handled in your bank, answer these important questions:

1. Who is responsible for placing the holds?

2. Where can I find out the date the customer's funds will be available? (some banks use availability calendars)

3. What do I need to do to ensure that the hold is placed or the check is flagged as a potential Regulation CC hold item?

4. What information is given to the customer when a hold is placed?

5. To whom can I refer customers if they have questions about Regulation CC?

SECTION 2: WITHDRAWALS AND CASHING CHECKS

Withdrawals from a Checking or Savings Account

Whether your customer is using a preprinted withdrawal form or a bank withdrawal form, the customer must enter the appropriate information, including:

- The amount of withdrawal in figures and words
- Signature made in the teller's presence to prevent forgery

Cashing a Check

Tellers must verify that all checks are negotiable, acceptable, and have a proper endorsement before processing the transaction.

Note: For detailed information on check negotiability, acceptability, and endorsement, see the *Handling Checks* module in this course.

Identification

It is imperative that tellers confirm the identity of anyone to whom they are giving out cash or information. A withdrawal completed or check cashed without adequate identification places the teller and the bank at great risk. You must

- Verify the identity of the person requesting the withdrawal, asking to cash a check, or asking for cash back from a deposit
- Be sure that the customer is legally entitled to withdraw funds from the account
- Ascertain that there are sufficient funds in the account

Counting Cash

If cash is to be disbursed, it should be counted at least twice. Many banks require tellers to count the cash three times.

- The first count is done as the cash is taken out of the cash drawer
- The second count is done to verify the amount before it is given to the customer. Often this count is entered into the teller's computer system to create a record of cash disbursed (cash-out). This computer record can be used when investigating discrepancies if a teller's cash is "off" when balancing at the end of the day
- The third count is done as the money is given to the customer

Note: For more information on cash counting methods, see the *Cash Handling* module in this course.

SECTION 3: TRANSACTON WORKFLOW

Where Does the Work Go?

During training, you learn many rules and procedures for carrying out your responsibilities. But how does your job fit into the corporate puzzle? Where does your day's work go when it leaves you? The following step-by-step outline and work flow diagram will help you see the big picture:

1. You receive transactions from customers
2. You accept and process these transactions, including checks
3. Transactions are sent to your bank's item processing department
4. Almost all checks processed are cleared as electronic check images
5. Checks are sorted according to whether they are drawn on your bank (on-us check) or a different bank
6. Smaller banks usually either deposit checks for clearing with a Federal Reserve Bank or with a correspondent bank. Larger banks deposit exclusively with a Federal Reserve Bank or use a combination of methods to clear checks

Exhibit 3-3 Work Flow

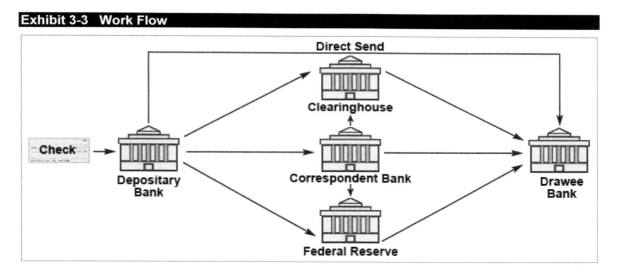

Your Job is Where Everything Begins

It is important to realize that your job is where everything begins. The quality of work you produce affects the ability of many other departments to do their jobs efficiently. The goals of all bank employees are the same: working together as a team to provide good customer service, follow sound banking practices, and remain profitable for your shareholders.

EXERCISE 3-2 HOW IS YOUR BANK ORGANIZED?

This exercise is designed to help you explore your bank's organizational structure so you will fully understand where your role fits into the operation of the bank. You will need to refer to your coworkers and your bank's materials that describe the various departments of your bank. After you complete the worksheet, review your answers with your supervisor and be sure to ask any additional questions you may have.

1. Draw an organization chart of the parent bank, showing the president by name, all the major departments reporting to the president, and the reporting channel through which your branch is linked to the president.

2. Draw an organization chart of your branch with the branch manager at the top and the title (not names) of all branch employees who report directly to the branch manager.

3. List other departments in the bank that are affected by what you do on a daily basis— for example, item processing, operations, and courier services.

4. Create a flow chart of what happens to the transactions you process throughout the day. Where do they go when they leave the branch?

SECTION 4: CHECK 21

When checks are scanned, a legally accepted digital image of the check is created. The paper reproduction of the image is called a substitute check, and they can be processed in the same way as the original check. The name "Check 21" is industry shorthand for the **Check Clearing for the 21st Century Act**. Check 21 allows for the creation of substitute checks from a check image.

Below are the legal requirements for substitute checks.

- Contain an image of the front and back of the original check
- Clearly state, "This is a legal copy of your check. You can use it the same way you would use the original check"
- Display a MICR (magnetic ink character recognition) line containing all the information appearing on the MICR line of the original check
- Conform in paper stock, dimension, and otherwise with generally applicable industry standards for substitute checks
- Be suitable for automated processing in the same manner as the original check

Because substitute checks are the legal equivalents of original paper checks, acceptance is mandatory. Every bank or person is required to treat substitute checks as if they were the original checks.

Note: Check with your supervisor to learn more about your bank's procedures for handling substitute checks at the teller line.

Exhibit 3-4   Substitute Check

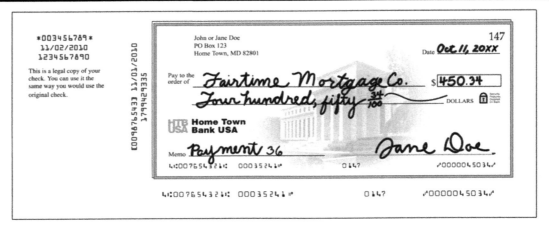

SECTION 5: NEGOTIABLE INSTRUMENTS

This section describes the guidelines for selling and cashing negotiable instruments guaranteed by banks, including official checks, money orders, and traveler's checks. "Guaranteed by banks" means that the bank selling the negotiable item guarantees that the item will be paid. Official checks (cashier's checks) are the most common type of negotiable item sold by banks.

Selling Negotiable Instruments

When selling negotiable instruments, remember to collect cash or guaranteed funds from the customer. Selling negotiable items is the same as handing the customer a stack of cash. Follow your bank's specific guidelines when issuing or cashing any of these products.

Cashing Money Orders

If a customer wishes to cash a money order drawn on another bank, follow the same guidelines as you would when cashing a check drawn on a bank other than your own.

One important security feature of money orders is that a maximum issue amount is printed somewhere on the face of the money order. Paying attention to this amount is critical when issuing as well as when cashing money orders.

For example, if you issue a money order for $600 and the face of the money order clearly states that the money order is not good for amounts over $500, your customer would suffer the consequences. The money order would be returned to the customer, who would have to come back to the bank to get two new money orders, one for $500 and another for $100.

Note: Refer to your bank's procedures for cashing money orders, as some banks do not offer this service.

Money orders are quite easy to duplicate and alter. One common con artist scam is to present an altered money order for an amount that is over the maximum issue amount.

Example

A new teller learned just how easy it is to alter money orders by firsthand experience. She was presented a money order for $1,500. She followed most of the steps required by her bank for cashing negotiable items. A few days later when the money order was returned as a stolen item, she learned from her supervisor how she had been fooled. Some imprinters punch out the amount of the money order in tiny holes across the face of the money order. The con artist who presented the money order had taken a straight pin and punched out a line in front of the 500. Had the new teller noticed the "not good for over $500" on the front of the money order she would have saved the bank a loss of $1,500.

The same con can be accomplished by using a pen with the same color ink as was used in the money order machine that printed the genuine money order. Now that sophisticated scanning equipment, desktop publishing software, and color printers are available, making highly sophisticated counterfeit money orders is easier than ever. ***Always follow your bank's procedures for cashing money orders very carefully.***

SECTION 6: LOAN PAYMENTS, BANKCARD TRANSACTIONS, AND FOREIGN CURRENCY

Your job as a teller may include transactions involving

- Installment and mortgage loan payments
- Bankcard cash advances
- Foreign currency

General guidelines for handling these transactions are described in this section. Be sure to check your bank's specific procedures for processing these transactions.

Installment and Mortgage Loan Payments

Installment loans (consumer loans) and mortgage loans have a fixed amount due on a specified payment date. If the payment is made after the due date, a late charge may be assessed if the normal grace period for payments has passed. This policy is often automatic with installment loans, but it may vary with mortgage loans.

Installment loans and mortgage loans usually have a 10- or 15-day grace period (often called a courtesy period) during which the customer may make the payment without incurring a late fee. After the grace period, the customer will be charged a late fee.

Overdue Loan Payments

You should know your bank's policy for accepting overdue payments, particularly those that are more than one or two months overdue. This is especially true for mortgage payments. You may be ordered to reject a mortgage payment unless its amount is for the entire sum of past due payments and penalty charges. The "reject payment" order would occur only after the bank had begun foreclosure action because of repeated nonpayment. Foreclosure is an unfortunate action taken only after all other negotiations and avenues of working out a suitable arrangement with the customer have failed. For this reason, accepting an overdue payment could place the bank in a disadvantageous legal position because the payment could stop the foreclosure process. The bank might then have to begin the often lengthy and costly foreclosure process again.

Bankcard Cash Advances

Bankcards allow customers to charge goods and services and to obtain cash advances from participating financial institutions. Customers can obtain cash advances at the teller windows of most banks. Cash advances are money loans for which the customer typically pays a finance charge and a transaction fee. The way finance charges are assessed on purchases varies among financial institutions. Some banks have a grace period during which a customer may pay without being assessed a finance charge. Finance charges generally apply on cash advances from the date of advance.

Occasionally the cash advance request will be refused. *Always follow the instructions given by the authorization center.* If the authorization center does not authorize the advance, return the customer's card. Sometimes the authorization center will instruct you to confiscate—and in some cases, destroy—the card. Before proceeding, involve your supervisor.

If the signature on the card and the signature on the form do not match, take both to your supervisor before processing the advance.

EXERCISE 3-3 BANKCARD CASH ADVANCES

1. Raymond Saul, a valuable, well-known customer, approaches your teller window. Mr. Saul says he would like a cash advance against his MasterCard for $250. The card was issued by a competing bank. Unfortunately, Rebecca Saul (Mr. Saul's wife) has his card in her purse. However, he has the card number.

    a. Can you complete a cash advance for Mr. Saul at this time? Why or why not?

    b. Mr. Saul says that Mrs. Saul will stop by later today and request the advance with his card. Is this possible? Explain.

2. Harold Steele, a noncustomer, requests a $100 cash advance against his Visa card. He has proper identification. When you call for an approval code, the authorization center says the card is stolen and tells you to cut it in two pieces and forward the pieces to the authorization office. Mr. Steele becomes enraged when you inform him. You have identification indicating Mr. Steele is who he says he is. Should you ignore the authorization center representative?

Caution: In situations where you feel physically threatened by a customer, do the safe thing. Try to calm him down by explaining that you will consult with your supervisor to see if there are some other options. Your supervisor will know what to say to this customer. In an extreme situation where the customer becomes so angry that he threatens you or others in the bank and will not agree to let you consult your supervisor, return the card to the customer so that he can leave the building. Then seek the assistance of a supervisor to determine what should be done.

Foreign Currency

Occasionally you may be asked to transact an exchange involving foreign currency. The customer may be a visitor from another country or one of your bank's customers wishing to send funds to a foreign country in that country's currency. Another customer may want to purchase foreign currency for foreign travel and sell back the unused amount afterward.

Does your bank handle foreign currency and drafts? If it does, the following general procedures will supplement your bank's regulations.

Some foreign currencies (not coins) can be exchanged in the United States. Most major countries exchange currencies on the world currency market. Check with your international representative at the time of the transaction for the current available rate. The currencies being traded could vary from day to day. Beware of foreign currency that may be unacceptable. Your bank may have books that illustrate commonly traded currencies.

A mathematical formula is used to convert a foreign currency amount to U.S. dollars. Because the value of currency changes frequently, it is critical to check today's exchange rate before using the formula.

Example

Mr. Blake wishes to exchange 540 Euros that were left over from his vacation. The current exchange rate in purchasing currency is 0.90 Euros to the U.S. dollar. There is a $5 noncustomer fee at your bank. Mr. Blake will receive U.S. $595 (540 ÷ .90 = $600 less $5 fee = $595).

Converting foreign currency is a complicated task, so be sure to ask for assistance.

SECTION 7: PROCESSING LARGE CASH TRANSACTIONS

In this section, you will learn when and how you must complete government-required documentation on large cash transactions. The form required by the federal government for these large cash transactions is called a Currency Transaction Report (CTR).

Currency Transaction Report (CTR)

The Bank Secrecy Act was enacted in 1970 and amended in 1986 by the Money Laundering Control Act (part of the Anti-Drug Abuse Act). The Money Laundering Control Act established money laundering as a federal crime.

Money laundering is the act of taking illegally obtained money (such as money obtained from drug sales) and converting it to assets that appear to have come from a legitimate source. Criminals try to use banks to "clean" illegally obtained funds.

Financial institutions are required to report each deposit, exchange of currency, currency withdrawal, or other payment or transfer that involves a **transaction in currency of *more* than $10,000**. Foreign currency should also be considered as cash and reported when the total exceeds $10,000 in U.S. currency. The Treasury Department provides a set of instructions with each CTR. It is very important that you read and follow these guidelines carefully.

When to Complete the CTR

The CTR must be completed in conjunction with the customer's transaction. If you have all the information necessary to complete the CTR, you may complete the form after you process the customer's transaction.

If the customer refuses to supply the necessary information (including identification and birth date), politely excuse yourself and get the assistance of your supervisor before completing the transaction. Many banks will refuse such transactions.

If the customer reduces the transaction amount to less than the $10,000 limit, check with your supervisor to see how your bank handles such situations.

Check your bank's policy about selling negotiable instruments such as cashier's checks. Some banks restrict their sale to noncustomers to less than $3,000.00, including the fee. Purchasing negotiable instruments is a common tactic used in money laundering. For example, a noncustomer comes to your window and wants to purchase a cashier's check with $9,500 in cash. Although this is below the $10,000 limit, the transaction is suspicious.

Note: All information on the CTR form is **required**, not optional. An individual who is an alien or not a resident of the United States is required to show a passport, alien identification card, or other official document showing nationality or residence. This information is documented on the CTR. After you complete the CTR, your supervisor will provide further instructions.

CTR Overview

Part I of the CTR form is for personal information about the person or persons involved in the transaction and the account numbers affected. In addition to entering the customer's name and address, you will be required to supply a social security or tax identification number and describe the identification you used to verify the customer. You will need to be as specific as possible when filling in the customer's occupation (exhibit 3-5).

Part II requires a description of the amount and type of transaction.

Part III requires information on your financial institution, such as the type of financial institution and the name and address.

Failure to report large currency transactions carries substantial penalties for both you and the bank. Talk with your supervisor about your bank's procedures for completing the CTR form.

Note: Exhibit 3-5 is a sample of the online CTR Form. This sample form is provided for training purposes only. Do not use the form for CTR filing purposes.

Exhibit 3-5 Sample CTR

Currency Transaction Report

Home	Step 1. Person Information	Step 2. Amount and Type of Transaction	Step 3. Financial Institution Information

SAMPLE

Currency Transaction Report
OMB No. 1506-0064

Version Number: 1.2

Steps to Submit

1. Complete the report in its entirety with all requested or required data known to the filer.
2. Click "Validate" to ensure proper formatting and that all required fields are completed.
3. Sign with PIN.
4. Click "Save"; filers may also "Print" a paper copy for their records.
5. Click "Submit".

Filing Name

*1 Type of filing   ☐ Initial report   ☐ Correct/amend prior report   ☐ FinCEN directed Backfiling

Prior report Document Control Number/BSA Identifier

Save	Validate	Print

By providing my PIN, I acknowledge that I am electronically signing the BSA report submitted.

Sign with PIN

Exhibit 3-5 continued

Currency Transaction Report

| Home | Step 1. Person Information | Step 2. Amount and Type of Transaction | Step 3. Financial Institution Information |

Part I Person Involved in Transaction 1 of 1 ⊕ ⊖

*2 a ☐ Person conducting transaction on own behalf   b ☐ Person conducting transaction for another   c ☐ Person on whose behalf transaction was conducted   d ☐ Courier Service (private)

3 ☐ Multiple transactions

Check ☐ If entity

*4 Individual's last name or entity's legal name   ☐ Unknown [_____]

*5 First name   ☐ Unknown [_____]

6 Middle name [_____]

Suffix [_____]

7 Gender [_____]

8 Alternate Name [_____]

9 Occupation or type of business [_____]

9a NAICS Code [_____]

*10 Address   ☐ Unknown [_____]

*11 City   ☐ Unknown [_____]

*12 State   ☐ Unknown [_____]   *13 ZIP/Postal Code ☐ Unknown [_____]

*14 Country   ☐ Unknown [_____]

*15 TIN   ☐ Unknown [_____]   16 TIN type [_____]

*17 Date of birth   ☐ Unknown [_____]

18 Contact phone number [_____]   Ext. [_____]

19 E-mail address [_____]

*20 Form of identification used to verify identity   ☐ Unknown

☐ Driver's license/State ID   ☐ Passport   ☐ Alien Registration   ☐ Other [_____]

Number [_____]   Country [_____]   Issuing State [_____]

21 Cash in amount for individual or entity listed in Item 4 $ _____

Account number [_____] ⊕ ⊖

22 Cash out amount for individual or entity listed in Item 4 $ _____

Account number [_____] ⊕ ⊖

Page 2 of 4

Exhibit 3-5 continued

Currency Transaction Report

Home	Step 1. Person Information	Step 2. Amount and Type of Transaction	Step 3. Financial Institution Information

Part II Amount and Type of Transaction(s). Check all boxes that apply.

*23 Date of transaction [ ]

24 ☐ Armored car (FI Contract)   ☐ ATM   ☐ Mail Deposit or Shipment   ☐ Night Deposit   ☐ Aggregated transactions

*25 CASH IN: (in U.S. dollar equivalent)		*27 CASH OUT: (in U.S. dollar equivalent)	
a Deposit(s)	$ _____ .00	a Withdrawal(s)	$ _____ .00
b Payment(s)	_____ .00	b Advance(s) on credit (including markers)	_____ .00
c Currency received for funds transfer(s) out	_____ .00	c Currency paid from funds transfer(s) in	_____ .00
d Purchase of negotiable instrument(s)	_____ .00	d Negotiable instrument(s) cashed	_____ .00
e Currency exchange(s)	_____ .00	e Currency exchange(s)	_____ .00
f Currency to prepaid access	_____ .00	f Currency from prepaid access	_____ .00
g Purchases of casinos chips, tokens and other gaming instruments	_____ .00	g Redemption(s) of casino chips, tokens, TITO tickets and other gaming instruments	_____ .00
h Currency wager(s) including money plays	_____ .00	h Payment(s) on wager(s) (including race and OTB or sports pool)	_____ .00
i Bills inserted into gaming devices	_____ .00	i Travel and complimentary expenses and book gaming incentives	_____ .00
z Other (specify):		j Payment for tournament, contest or other promotions	_____ .00
_____	_____ .00	z Other (specify): _____	_____ .00
Total Cash in	$ _____ .00	Total Cash out	$ _____ .00

26 Foreign Cash in _____   Foreign Country [ ]   ⊕ ⊖

28 Foreign Cash out _____   Foreign Country [ ]   ⊕ ⊖

Page 3 of 4

Exhibit 3-5   continued

Currency Transaction Report

Home	Step 1. Person Information	Step 2. Amount and Type of Transaction	Step 3. Financial Institution Information

Part III Financial Institution Where Transaction(s) Takes Place 1   of 1   ⊕ ⊖

*37 Type of financial institution

       Other (specify)

*29 Primary federal regulator

38 If 37a - Casino/Card Club is checked, indicate type (check only one)

☐ State licensed casino   ☐ Tribal authorized casino   ☐ Card club   ☐ Other

*30 Legal name of financial institution

31 Alternate name, e.g. trade name, DBA

*32 EIN

*33 Address

*34 City

*35 State

*36 ZIP Code

39 Financial institution ID type

       ID number

*40 Contact office

*41 Phone number   Ext.

*42   Date Filed   (Date filed will be auto-populated when the form is signed.)

Page 4 of 4

CTR Terminology

Here are some terms associated with CTRs that you should discuss in detail with your supervisor.

Large currency transactions. Any withdrawal, deposit, currency exchange, or purchase of a negotiable item involving more than $10,000 in currency in one business day.

Multiple transactions. More than one transaction on the same business day made by or on behalf of the same person that total more than $10,000 in currency. Deposits made at night, over the weekend, or on a holiday are considered transactions of the next business day following the day of the deposit. Thus, a deposit of $5,000 made on Saturday and a deposit of $6,000 made on Monday would total a $11,000 transaction on Monday. Because this exceeds the $10,000 limit, your teller system should flag the deposit on Monday as requiring a CTR.

Exempt transactions. Customers, identified by your bank's regulatory management department, whose normal course of business meets certain eligibility requirements are exempt from having to complete a CTR for their normal business transaction. The exemptions process is generally handled by your bank's Bank Security Act (BSA) department because certain businesses are not eligible for exemption due to the nature of their activity.

Record of purchase of monetary instruments. Banks are required to keep information regarding the identity of individuals using cash to purchase such monetary instruments as official bank checks (cashier's checks), money orders, and traveler's checks in the amount of $3,000 through $10,000.

Completing a CTR Form

The key to Currency Transaction Reporting is to remember that **any cash transaction or multiple transactions by your customer that exceed $10,000** *must* **be reported.** Here are a few examples to help you understand reportable transactions.

Individual transaction:

Your customer Jerry Maxwell withdraws $11,000 in cash from his savings account. He then hands back $3,000 in cash to be deposited to his checking account.

Would you report Jerry's transactions?

ANSWER: You would report the $11,000 transaction but not the $3,000 transaction. Even though the net amount of cash Jerry is receiving is only $8,000, he completed a cash transaction (the savings withdrawal) that exceeded the $10,000 amount.

Multiple transactions:

Your customer, Alice Kramer, owns a sole proprietorship business and deposits $15,000 in cash into her business checking account and then withdraws $12,000 cash from her business savings account.

Would you report Alice's transaction?

ANSWER: You would, in fact, report both of Alice's transactions. You would report a cash in of $15,000 and a cash out of $12,000. Cash ins and outs are never aggregated (added together or netted out) for CTR reporting purposes.

Employee completing a transaction for a business:

Linda Lane is an employee of Apple Grocery Store. Every Monday morning she brings in a large cash deposit for the store. Anytown Bank has elected to complete CTR forms on all large currency transactions. This week's deposit for Apple Grocery Store includes $18,500 in cash.

Since this is not a deposit of Linda's personal account, would you report the transaction?

ANSWER: Even though Linda is not depositing her own funds, the cash amount dictates that a CTR form be completed. In this situation, you would check item 2(b) of Part I because Linda is conducting a transaction for another individual or entity.

EXERCISE 3-4   LARGE CASH TRANSACTIONS

Place a check mark next to the situations that would require completion of a CTR form.

☐ 1.   Customer wants to exchange $12,000 in $20 bills for the same amount in $100 dollar bills

☐ 2.   Customer buys $2,000 in traveler's checks with cash

☐ 3.   Customer deposits $5,133.27 in cash

☐ 4.   Customer wants to cash a check for $10,100 and receive large bills

☐ 5.   Customer purchases a $14,500 cashier's check using a check from his personal account

Suspicious Activity Report (SAR)

In addition to reporting large cash transactions on a Currency Transaction Report (CTR), part of your responsibility as a teller is to be aware of activity that seems to be suspicious.

An obvious example of reportable suspicious activity would be a customer who begins an $11,000 transaction but then reduces the amount when told about the CTR.

Other examples of suspicious activity would include:

- Corporate accounts where deposits or withdrawals are made primarily in cash rather than with checks and the business is not a cash-intensive business (a CPA firm, for example, would not be expected to make large cash deposits, but a gas station would)
- Small businesses that frequently make cash deposits consisting only of $50 bills or $100 bills
- Businesses that have only one location but make deposits at several branches of your bank, especially if the branches are not close to the business
- Deposits of sequentially numbered cashier's checks or money orders
- Large amounts of cash deposited that are wrapped with the currency straps from another bank
- Customers who frequently go to a safe deposit box before making cash deposits that are less than the reportable dollar amount
- Customers who make several cash deposits through an ATM—and each deposit is below the reportable dollar amount
- Customers who are reluctant to provide personal information or information about their businesses
- Customers who have no record of past or present employment but frequently make large transactions
- Customers who conduct banking activity that is inconsistent with their business; i.e. a veterinarian who frequently makes deposits with lots of small bills, or a teacher who frequently deposits large cashier's checks

Note: In situations such as these, a Suspicious Activity Report (SAR) must be completed. Unlike the Currency Transaction Reports, SARs report suspicious activity that involves checks as well as cash (exhibit 3-6).

Do not discuss a Suspicious Activity Report with a customer or even inform the customer that you are filing the report. Check with your supervisor to see how Suspicious Activity Reports are handled in your bank.

In general, tellers usually do not file SARs. Tellers should consider reporting suspicious activity to the bank's responsible person when:

- The amount in question totals at least $5,000 and the transaction appears unusual for the customer or business; e.g., a CPA firm depositing large amounts of cash is more suspicious than a mom and pop grocery store doing the same
- The bank suspects that the funds involved in the transaction have been obtained from illegal activities
- The transaction seems unusual or peculiar for the customer or the business the customer represents (note that this condition alone is not enough to file a SAR)
- The transaction appears to be deliberately structured to avoid any Bank Secrecy Act reporting requirements. Further, if the transaction involves employee malfeasance (of any amount; there is no threshold for such instances), you should report such activity to the appropriate individual at your bank

Do not let anyone at the bank talk you out of reporting suspicious activity. If you note something that appears to you to be unusual or suspicious, report it—even if someone "knows" the customer and states that "they do this all the time." Just because someone else does not view an activity or a transaction as suspicious does not mean that you should ignore your own best judgment. In fact, you are required by law to report. If the person investigating the activity determines that it is not suspicious, a SAR will not be filed, but you do not hurt yourself or incur any penalty for reporting.

Note: Exhibit 3-6 is a sample of the online SAR Form. This sample form is provided for training purposes only. Do not use the form for SAR filing purposes.

When Both a CTR and SAR Must Be Completed

At times, a bank may need to complete both a CTR and a SAR for a transaction. If a currency transaction exceeds $10,000 and is suspicious, the bank must file both a CTR and a SAR. If a currency transaction equals or is less than $10,000 and is suspicious, the bank should file only a Suspicious Activity Report.

Important: Check with your supervisor when you have any questions about when a CTR and/or SAR should be completed.

Exhibit 3-6 Sample Suspicious Activity Report

Suspicious Activity Report

Home	Step 1. Filing Institution Contact Information	Step 2. Financial Institution Where Activity Occurred	Step 3. Subject Information	Step 4. Suspicious Activity Information	Step 5. Narrative

SAMPLE

Suspicious Activity Report
OMB No. 1506-0065

Version Number: 1.1

Steps to Submit

1. Complete the report in its entirety with all requested or required data known to the filer.
2. Click "Validate" to ensure proper formatting and that all required fields are completed.
3. Sign with PIN.
4. Click "Save"; filers may also "Print" a paper copy for their records.
5. Click "Submit".

Filing name _____

*1 Type of filing
(Check all that apply)

☐ Initial report   ☐ Correct/Amend prior report

☐ Continuing activity report   ☐ Joint report

Prior report Document Control Number/BSA Identifier _____

Attachment _____

By providing my PIN, I acknowledge that I am electronically signing the BSA report submitted.

Sign with PIN	This PDF is an example only. Please do not use it in a production environment.

Page 1 of 7

Exhibit 3-6   continued

Suspicious Activity Report

Home	Step 1. Filing Institution Contact Information	Step 2. Financial Institution Where Activity Occurred	Step 3. Subject Information	Step 4. Suspicious Activity Information	Step 5. Narrative

Part IV Filing Institution Contact Information

*82 Type of financial institution

*78 Primary federal regulator

*79 Filer name (Holding company, lead financial institution, or agency, if applicable)

*80 TIN   *81 TIN type

83 Type of Securities and Futures institution or individual filing this report - check box(es) for functions that apply to this report

☐ Clearing broker-securities   ☐ Introducing broker-securities   ☐ SRO Securities
☐ CPO/CTA   ☐ Investment Adviser   ☐ Subsidiary of financial/bank holding company
☐ Futures Commission Merchant   ☐ Investment company   ☐ Other
☐ Holding company   ☐ Retail foreign exchange dealer
☐ Introducing broker-commodities   ☐ SRO Futures

84 Financial institution identification   Type

Number

*85 Address

*86 City

*87 State   *88 ZIP/Postal Code   *89 Country

90 Alternate name, e.g., AKA - individual or trade name, DBA - entity

91 Internal control/file number

92 LE contact agency

93 LE contact name

94 LE contact phone number (Include Area Code)   Ext.

95 LE contact date

*96 Filing institution contact office

*97 Filing institution contact phone number (Include Area Code)   Ext.

98 Date filed   (Date filed will be auto-populated when the form is signed.)

Page 2 of 7

Exhibit 3-6 continued

Suspicious Activity Report

Home	Step 1. Filing Institution Contact Information	Step 2. Financial Institution Where Activity Occurred	Step 3. Subject Information	Step 4. Suspicious Activity Information	Step 5. Narrative

Part III Information about Financial Institution Where Activity Occurred   1   of   1

*47 Type of financial institution

*48 Primary federal regulator

49 Type of gaming institution

☐ State licensed casino   ☐ Tribal authorized casino   ☐ Card club   ☐ Other (specify)

50 Type of Securities and Futures institution or individual where activity occurred - check box(es) that apply to this report

☐ Clearing broker-securities   ☐ Introducing broker-securities   ☐ Subsidiary of financial/bank holding company

☐ Futures Commission Merchant   ☐ Investment Adviser   ☐ Other

☐ Holding company   ☐ Investment company

☐ Introducing broker-commodities   ☐ Retail foreign exchange dealer

51 Financial institution identification   Type

Number

52 Financial institution's role in transaction   ☐ Selling location   ☐ Paying location   ☐ Both

*53 Legal name of financial institution   ☐ Unknown

54 Alternate Name, e.g., AKA - individual or trade name, DBA - entity

*55 TIN   ☐ Unknown   56 TIN type

*57 Address   ☐ Unknown

*58 City   ☐ Unknown

59 State

*60 ZIP/Postal Code   ☐ Unknown

*61 Country   ☐ Unknown

62 Internal control/file number

63 Loss to financial institution $ _____ .00

Branch where activity occurred information   If no branch activity involved, check this box ☐

Branch Information

64 Branch's role in transaction   ☐ Selling location   ☐ Paying location   ☐ Both

65 Address of branch or office where activity occurred

67 City   66 RSSD Number

68 State   69 ZIP/Postal Code   *70 Country

Page 3 of 7

Exhibit 3-6   continued

Suspicious Activity Report

Home	Step 1. Filing Institution Contact Information	Step 2. Financial Institution Where Activity Occurred	Step 3. Subject Information	Step 4. Suspicious Activity Information	Step 5. Narrative

Part I Subject Information   1   of   1

2 Check: ☐ if entity,   ☐ if all critical* subject information is unavailable (Does not include item 24)

*3 Individual's last name or entity's legal name ☐ Unknown

*4 First name ☐ Unknown

5 Middle name/initial

Suffix   Gender

*16 Date of birth ☐ Unknown

6 Alternate name, e.g., AKA - individual or trade name, DBA - entity

7 Occupation or type of business

7a NAICS Code

*13 TIN ☐ Unknown   14 TIN type

18 Phone number   Ext.   17 Type

19 E-mail address

19a Website (URL) address

20 Corroborative statement to filer?   25 Subject's role in suspicious activity

Subject Address Information

*8 Address ☐ Unknown

*9 City ☐ Unknown

*10 State ☐ Unknown   *11 ZIP/Postal Code ☐ Unknown

*12 Country ☐ Unknown

*15 Form of identification for subject   Unknown ☐

Type

Number   Issuing State   Country

21 Relationship of the subject to an institution listed in Part III or IV (check all that apply)

a Institution TIN

b ☐ Accountant   e ☐ Attorney   h ☐ Director   k ☐ Officer
c ☐ Agent   f ☐ Borrower   i ☐ Employee   l ☐ Owner or Controlling Shareholder
d ☐ Appraiser   g ☐ Customer   j ☐ No relationship to institution   z ☐ Other

22 Status of relationship   23 Action date

*24 Financial institution TIN and account number(s) affected that are related to subject   No known accounts involved ☐

Institution TIN   ☐ Non-US Financial Institution

account number   Closed? Yes ☐

Page 4 of 7

Exhibit 3-6 continued

Suspicious Activity Report

Home	Step 1. Filing Institution Contact Information	Step 2. Financial Institution Where Activity Occurred	Step 3. Subject Information	Step 4. Suspicious Activity Information	Step 5. Narrative

Part II Suspicious Activity Information

*26 Amount involved in this report ☐ Amount Unknown ☐ No amount involved $ _____ .00

*27 Date or date range of suspicious activity for this report From _____ To _____

28 Cumulative amount (only applicable when "Continuing activity report" is checked in Item 1) $ _____ .00

When completing item 29 through 38, check all that apply

29 Structuring
a ☐ Alters transaction to avoid BSA recordkeeping requirement
b ☐ Alters transaction to avoid CTR requirement
c ☐ Customer cancels transaction to avoid BSA reporting and recordkeeping requirements
d ☐ Multiple transactions below BSA recordkeeping threshold
e ☐ Multiple transactions below CTR threshold
f ☐ Suspicious inquiry by customer regarding BSA reporting or recordkeeping requirements
z ☐ Other _____

30 Terrorist Financing
a ☐ Known or suspected terrorist/terrorist organization
z ☐ Other _____

31 Fraud (Type)
a ☐ ACH
b ☐ Business loan
c ☐ Check
d ☐ Consumer loan
e ☐ Credit/Debit card
f ☐ Healthcare
g ☐ Mail
h ☐ Mass-marketing
i ☐ Pyramid scheme
j ☐ Wire
z ☐ Other _____

32 Casinos
a ☐ Inquiry about end of business day
b ☐ Minimal gaming with large transactions
c ☐ Suspicious intra-casino funds transfers
d ☐ Suspicious use of counter checks or markers
z ☐ Other _____

33 Money Laundering
a ☐ Exchange small bills for large bills or vice versa
b ☐ Suspicion concerning the physical condition of funds
c ☐ Suspicion concerning the source of funds
d ☐ Suspicious designation of beneficiaries, assignees or joint owners
e ☐ Suspicious EFT/wire transfers
f ☐ Suspicious exchange of currencies
g ☐ Suspicious receipt of government payments/benefits
h ☐ Suspicious use of multiple accounts
i ☐ Suspicious use of noncash monetary instruments
j ☐ Suspicious use of third-party transactors (straw-man)
k ☐ Trade Based Money Laundering/Black Market Peso Exchange
l ☐ Transaction out of pattern for customer(s)
z ☐ Other _____

34 Identification/Documentation
a ☐ Changes spelling or arrangement of name
b ☐ Multiple individuals with same or similar identities
c ☐ Provided questionable or false documentation
d ☐ Refused or avoided request for documentation
e ☐ Single individual with multiple identities
z ☐ Other _____

35 Other Suspicious Activities
a ☐ Account takeover
b ☐ Bribery or gratuity
c ☐ Counterfeit instruments
d ☐ Elder financial exploitation
e ☐ Embezzlement/theft/disappearance of funds
f ☐ Forgeries
g ☐ Identity theft
h ☐ Little or no concern for product performance penalties, fees, or tax consequences
i ☐ Misuse of "free look"/cooling-off/right of rescission
j ☐ Misuse of position or self-dealing
k ☐ Suspected public/private corruption (domestic)
l ☐ Suspected public/private corruption (foreign)
m ☐ Suspicious use of informal value transfer system
n ☐ Suspicious use of multiple transaction locations
o ☐ Transaction with no apparent economic, business, or lawful purpose
p ☐ Two or more individuals working together
q ☐ Unauthorized electronic intrusion
r ☐ Unlicensed or unregistered MSB
z ☐ Other _____

Page 5 of 7

Exhibit 3-6   continued

Suspicious Activity Report

Home	Step 1. Filing Institution Contact Information	Step 2. Financial Institution Where Activity Occurred	Step 3. Subject Information	Step 4. Suspicious Activity Information	Step 5. Narrative

36 Insurance

- a ☐ Excessive insurance
- b ☐ Excessive or unusal cash borrowing against policy/annuity
- c ☐ Proceeds sent to or received from unrelated third party
- d ☐ Suspicious life settlement sales insurance (e.g.,STOLI's, *Viaticals*)

- e ☐ Suspicious termination of policy or contract
- f ☐ Unclear or no insurable interest
- z ☐ Other [＿＿＿＿＿＿＿＿＿＿＿＿]

37 Securities/Futures/Options

- a ☐ Insider trading
- b ☐ Market manipulation/wash trading
- c ☐ Misappropriation

- d ☐ Unauthorized pooling
- z ☐ Other [＿＿＿＿＿＿＿＿＿＿＿＿]

38 Mortgage Fraud

- a ☐ Appraisal fraud
- b ☐ Foreclosure fraud
- c ☐ Loan Modification fraud

- d ☐ Reverse mortgage fraud
- z ☐ Other [＿＿＿＿＿＿＿＿＿＿＿＿]

39 Were any of the following product type(s) involved in the suspicious activity? (Check all that apply)

- a ☐ Bonds/Notes
- b ☐ Commercial mortgage
- c ☐ Commercial paper
- d ☐ Credit card
- e ☐ Debit card
- f ☐ Forex transactions

- g ☐ Futures/Options on futures
- h ☐ Hedge fund
- i ☐ Home equity loan
- j ☐ Home equity line of credit
- k ☐ Insurance/Annuity products
- l ☐ Mutual fund

- m ☐ Options on securities
- n ☐ Penny stocks/Microcap securities
- o ☐ Prepaid access
- p ☐ Residential mortgage
- q ☐ Security futures products
- r ☐ Stocks

- s ☐ Swap, hybrid, or other derivatives
- z ☐ Other (List below) [＿＿＿＿＿＿＿]

40 Were any of the following instrument type(s)/payment mechanism(s) involved in the suspicious activity? (Check all that apply)

- a ☐ Bank/Cashier's check
- b ☐ Foreign currency
- c ☐ Funds transfer

- d ☐ Gaming instruments
- e ☐ Government payment
- f ☐ Money orders

- g ☐ Personal/Business check
- h ☐ Travelers checks
- i ☐ U.S. Currency

- z ☐ Other (List below) [＿＿＿＿＿＿＿]

41 Commodity type (If applicable)

[＿＿＿＿＿＿＿＿＿＿＿＿＿＿＿＿＿＿＿＿＿]

42 Product/Instrument description (If needed)

[＿＿＿＿＿＿＿＿＿＿＿＿＿＿＿＿＿＿＿＿＿]

43 Market where traded ⓘ

[＿＿＿＿＿＿＿]

44 IP address (If available)

[＿＿＿＿＿＿＿＿＿＿＿＿＿]

45 CUSIP® number

[＿＿＿＿＿＿＿]

Page 6 of 7

Exhibit 3-6 continued

Suspicious Activity Report

Home	Step 1. Filing Institution Contact Information	Step 2. Financial Institution Where Activity Occurred	Step 3. Subject Information	Step 4. Suspicious Activity Information	Step 5. Narrative

Part V   Suspicious Activity Information - Narrative*

Page 7 of 7

SECTION 8: SECURITY WHEN PROCESSING TRANSACTIONS

In this section, you will learn about security procedures to protect you and the bank.

New Accounts

A new account must be treated carefully because the new customer does not have a history with the bank and therefore must establish one. There is no reason to suspect every new customer. However, the potential for fraud is greater with new, unestablished customers.

During the time an account is defined as "new" (for most banks this is 30 days), tellers must adhere to the following rules and regulations.

- **Stay alert to any unusual activity**, such as frequent deposits or, large and/or frequent cash deposits.
- **Know your bank's policy** and security precautions for processing deposits for new customers.
- **Check the customer's identification** every time a check is cashed or money is withdrawn.
- **Strictly enforce your bank's rules** for acceptable identification used by customers completing transactions.

Dual Control

Most transactions between a teller and customer are conducted one-on-one, with the teller processing the transaction. However, some types of transactions require two individuals working together—a security technique known as dual control.

Dual control protects the teller from being blamed if funds are missing. The following transactions are generally processed under dual control:

- Processing large amounts of cash (for example, a vault cash delivery from an armored car service)
- Loading funds into an ATM
- Processing night deposit bags or ATM deposits
- Counting vault cash

EXERCISE 3-5 NEW ACCOUNTS

1. Why should a new account be treated carefully?

2. Name at least three precautions you should take with regard to new accounts.

3. What are your bank's policies on cashing checks on new accounts?

Deposits with Cash Back

Deposits with cash back (or "less cash") occur when a customer wants to deposit a check into an account, but would like a portion of the amount deposited in cash. For example, Mr. James has received a check for $3,500. He would like to place $3,000 into his savings account and would like $500 cash back.

The significance of the deposit with cash back relates to security and the possibility of a forged or altered check being drawn against insufficient funds, thereby exposing the bank to financial loss.

The perpetrator of this type of deposit fraud hopes the teller will relax bank procedures because the majority of the check is deposited. Tellers are tempted to assume a check must be good when a customer requests only a small portion of its value in cash.

When you are presented with a deposit that includes cash back, be very careful to follow your bank's policies about examining checks for forgery or alteration and verifying the identification of your customer.

Remember to use the following precautions when processing deposits with cash back:

1. Carefully examine every check to ensure it is genuine and unaltered
2. Know your customers
   - Ask for identification if you do not know them
   - Verify their signature using the ID or signature card
3. Verify that the account the check is being deposited into is the correct account
4. Verify that the account balance is sufficient to cover the cash amount
5. Always ask yourself, "Would I cash this check if no deposit were being made?"

Note: Rule of thumb—*anytime* you are handing cash over to a customer you should verify and record an acceptable form of identification.

Case Study: Deposit Fraud

Read the following scenario and be prepared to discuss what Elizabeth could have done to prevent this deposit swindle.

It is Monday morning after a three-day weekend, and the bank is very busy. The teller line is quite long and all of the tellers, including Elizabeth, are trying to process transactions as quickly as possible for their customers.

A man walks up to Elizabeth and greets her warmly, "Hi Elizabeth! Boy you guys are sure busy today. I don't think I've been in here when the lines were so long. I guess three-day weekends take a toll on you guys, don't they?" He asks for a deposit slip. He fills out the deposit slip and hands it to Elizabeth. She notices that the customer's name is Marcus White. As Elizabeth looks at the deposit, Marcus continues to involve her in a friendly conversation about his activities over the weekend.

Elizabeth doesn't recognize Marcus, but assumes she must have helped him in the past, since he knows her name.

Elizabeth notes that Marcus is depositing a check in the amount of $2,300. He is requesting $350 cash back.

Elizabeth pulls up Marcus' account and sees that he does most of his banking through the ATM. She also sees that he has $3,000 available in his account—enough to cover the $350 cash amount he is requesting. So, she counts the money out of her drawer, counts it out to Marcus, thanks him for his business, and tells him to have a great day.

Three days later the check Marcus deposited is returned as being drawn on a closed account.

Six days later a gentleman walks up to Elizabeth's window. He shows her a notice that a check has been returned on his account and says he did not deposit a check for that amount. Elizabeth asks for his account number. When she pulls up the account, Elizabeth is shocked to discover the name on the account is Marcus White—but the gentleman standing in front of her is not the same one who deposited the check and got cash back.

Elizabeth realizes she is the victim of deposit fraud.

Con artists use the names and account numbers of bank customers to perpetrate deposit fraud. How do these thieves get the name and account number? Typically, from stealing checks from mailboxes or purses left in parked cars. Checks provide the customer's name, bank name, and account number.

With such information, a con artist simply walks into a branch of the victim's bank, probably not in the victim's own neighborhood, asks for a counter deposit slip, and makes a deposit that includes cash back. Deception is the con artist's most effective weapon. With a name, an account number, and the ability to appear confident, a con artist has all that is needed to walk out of a bank with cash in his pocket.

Later the checks will be returned as stolen items. The con artist is long gone and the bank is left with a loss.

EXERCISE 3-6 DEPOSIT FRAUD

1. What one precaution could Elizabeth have taken to prevent this deposit fraud from happening?

2. What did "Marcus" do to make Elizabeth feel more comfortable and relaxed with him?

3. Summarize what you have learned about how a deposit with cash back should be handled.

4. At your own bank, what would be the consequences for this violation of procedures? Probation? Termination?

Check Kiting

Another scheme used by con artists and sometimes even legitimate businesses that have run into difficult times is called kiting. Check kiting schemes are designed to obtain cash from bank checking accounts that appear to have funds available but in fact do not have funds to cover the withdrawals.

In a typical kiting swindle, a person uses several accounts in different banks to draw against nonexistent balances. Check kiting can become very complicated and confusing, but it often follows this basic sequence of events:

1. The customer opens several checking accounts in different banks, often scattered around the country. These accounts might be opened with a cashier's check or with cash to minimize or eliminate the hold time
2. Additional accounts are then opened at nearby banks
3. Checks are then quickly written to transfer funds from one account to another, frequently getting cash back or withdrawing all the funds the next business day, when the funds are available, but the depositing bank does not know if the check will clear or not. These transfers from account to account occur so frequently that no actual funds are in the account when a check is written against it
4. The check writer usually skips town with more money than has been deposited

Check kiting works because, in the check collection process, funds remain uncollected for a period of days until the check clears; then the checks are deemed collected (or cleared). This process is called the check "float." Because of federal Regulation CC requirements and also because of their own policies, many banks make funds available to customers before the kited checks have had a chance to circulate back to the drawee bank (check writer's bank) as uncollectible.

Kiting is made easier by tellers who mistakenly trust the kiter and fail to put a hold on the account (where permitted). Businesses that may have fallen on hard times sometimes open additional accounts at other banks in order to use this float time to stall payment of checks written for payroll or supplies. The business is hoping to receive payment from one of their customers for a completed job in time to cover the outstanding checks.

A typical example of check kiting goes as follows:

1. The customer deposits $1,000 cash in bank A
2. Using bank A checks, the customer makes three separate $900 deposits in banks B, C, and D off of the same $1,000 deposit
3. Before these three $900 checks are cleared, the customer cashes checks for $700 each at banks B, C, and D, leaving a balance in each account to avoid suspicion
4. Still before the three $700 checks are cleared, the customer returns to bank A and closes out the original $1,000 account. For a brief investment of $1,000 (the amount

temporarily deposited in bank A), this check kiter made a return of $2,100 (the three $700 checks cashed at banks B, C, and D

This all happens within a few days' time.

If you notice an account with a lot of checks drawn on other banks with your customer as the check writer, notify your supervisor immediately. Someone intentionally trying to deceive the bank is not a good customer; therefore, any relationship with that customer should be terminated. Following the bank's policy on placing holds and being alert to unusual transactions are the best ways to stop check kiting.

Always be alert for the following four warning signals of check kiting:

1. Excessive activity in an account, such as many checks being cashed in a short period or frequent customer inquiries about the balance
2. Large deposits and large withdrawals
3. Deposits involving checks written on the depositor's accounts in other banks
4. Deposits by checks drawn on another bank and bearing low check numbers. This combination of factors indicates a new and potentially unstable account

Use the following procedures to prevent check kiting:

- Follow normal check-cashing procedures
- Do not cash checks drawn against uncollected funds
- Do not deviate from routine identification procedures
- Report any suspicions about possible check fraud to your supervisor
- Do not accuse anyone of check fraud

EXERCISE 3-7 CHECK KITING

1. What is check kiting? How is it done?

2. What are the four warning signals of a check kiting scheme?

3. What four steps can tellers take to prevent check kiters?

Fraudulent Cashier's Checks

Because of a rash of scams involving fraudulent cashier's checks sent to individuals, banks have to be especially cautious to protect their customers and also their own reputations. The scams vary, but usually begin with someone offering to

- Buy something an individual advertised for sale
- Pay an individual to work at home
- Give an individual an "advance" on a sweepstakes he has "won"
- Give an individual the first installment on the millions to be received for agreeing to transfer money in a foreign country to his bank account for safekeeping
- Become romantically involved

Usually the scammer sends an "excess" amount to the victim. Perhaps the "buyers" have sent a check for more than the advertised price and asked the seller to send the excess money to someone else, often in a foreign country, because it is too difficult for the buyer to send the funds directly to the person in the foreign country. Or the scammer notifies his victim that he has won a "lottery" but must pay taxes on the winnings. In some cases, the scammer claims to be "wiring" money into an account, when in fact he has simply mailed a counterfeit check to be deposited into the victim's bank account, so that it appears to the victim that the "wired" money has arrived. The victims are often told not to disclose the details or circumstances to anyone, including the bank.

Fraudsters make the checks sent to victims appear to be genuine. They may very closely imitate genuine cashier's checks of legitimate banks. In some cases, the counterfeit checks use valid account numbers at another bank. In many cases, it is very difficult for anyone, including a teller, to detect that the check is counterfeit. The forgeries are of excellent quality. In addition, it is not feasible—or necessarily helpful—to try to verify with the bank on which the check appears to be drawn. In some cases, phone numbers or websites are provided to "verify" that the check is good and the victim is entitled to the funds.

At some point, the scammer attempts to persuade the victim to withdraw the excess funds and wire them to pay some sort of fee or taxes. The key here is that there is a request to wire the funds.

This is where tellers may get involved. If a customer asks when the check will be cleared, the teller should explain to the customer that while funds will be available on a certain date, that does not mean the check is good. The teller should make clear that the check could still be returned and that the customer is responsible for any funds withdrawn. Also, where appropriate, if a customer asks whether a check is "good," the teller should make further inquiries about the source of the check. References by the customer to lotteries, internet sales, and wiring funds to foreign countries should raise red flags, and the teller should get the attention of a supervisor.

MODULE 3 REVIEW QUIZ

1. Mr. Thompson is a long-time customer of the bank. He comes in every week to make a deposit to his savings account. In reviewing the deposit slip, you notice that the amount of the check is different than what Mr. Thompson has listed on the deposit slip. What should be your next step in this transaction?

2. If a customer wants to exchange $17,000 worth of $100 bills for $20 bills, what should you do?

3. At your bank, installment loans have a 30-day grace period. Mrs. Dewhurst brings her car loan payment in 15 days into the grace period. Will Mrs. Dewhurst have to pay a late fee to your bank?

4. A cash advance against a bankcard is a money loan for which the customer must repay the principal advance amount plus which two fees?

    a. finance charge
    b. origination fee
    c. closing fee
    d. transaction fee

5. Can you exchange foreign currency for noncustomers at your bank?

6. What can a teller do to prevent deposit fraud?

7. What does a check kiter hope to accomplish?

8. Your customer wants to deposit a cashier's check in the amount of $9,000 and use the funds to wire $1,500 to someone in another country. The customer asks you if the check is "good." What should you tell the customer?

ANSWERS TO EXERCISES

Exercise 3-1: Regulation CC

1. Establish maximum check-hold periods. Require disclosures to customers. Give the Federal Reserve Board authority to improve the check-clearing system.
2. Within one and one-half inches from the trailing edge of the check in the area indicated on the back.
3. Answers vary according to bank policy.

Exercise 3-3: Bankcard Cash Advances

1a. No. He must have the card with him for you to process the cash advance.

1b. A cash advance should only be processed for the person whose name appears on the card. Explaining bank policy will probably not be enough to satisfy Mr. Saul. Explore what other options are available to see that Mr. Saul gets the cash he needs. Check with your bank manager to see if an exception can be made for the Sauls, since they are valuable long-time customers.

2. No, you must follow the instructions of the card center and destroy the card. Before proceeding, involve your supervisor.

Exercise 3-4: Large Cash Transactions

1. **Customer wants to exchange $12,000 in 20s for 100s**
2. Customer buys $2,000 in traveler's checks with cash
3. Customer purchases cashier's check for $5,133.27 with cash
4. **Customer wants to cash check for $10,100 and receive large bills**
5. Customer purchases a $14,500 cashier's check using a check from his personal account

Exercise 3-5: New Accounts

1. New customers are not known to the bank.
2. Stay alert to any unusual activity. Know your responsibilities for following security procedures. Check ID carefully every time a check is cashed or money is withdrawn. Follow bank procedures on what is considered acceptable ID.
3. Answers vary from bank to bank.

Exercise 3-6: Deposit Fraud

1. As precautions, Elizabeth could have requested identification from the person presenting the deposit and check. Elizabeth verified that Marcus White did have an account, but she failed to verify that the individual standing in front of her was in fact Marcus White

2. Marcus engaged Elizabeth in friendly small talk to make her feel more comfortable about processing his transaction. The bank was also very busy, and everyone was rushing to accommodate the long lines. He created the impression that he was in the branch often, "I don't think I've been in here when the lines were so long." He also used a counter deposit slip rather than a preprinted one

3. Cash back from a deposit slip should be treated in the same way as a check being presented for cash. You should ask for identification. Most losses of this type occur during hectic, busy times in the bank. Most losses occur because a teller did not follow the procedures of his or her bank

4. Answers will vary

Exercise 3-7: Check Kiting

1. Check kiting is fraudulent activity designed to obtain cash from accounts that do not have sufficient cash to cover the withdrawals. The customer opens one account with cash or a cashier's check. Additional accounts are opened at other banks using checks drawn off of the first bank. Then checks are written transferring funds between banks until the kiter has manipulated nonexistent funds into a cash gain

2. Four warning signals of a check kiting scheme are: (1) excessive activity in an account; (2) large deposits and large withdrawals; (3) deposits involving checks written on the depositor's accounts in other banks; and (4) deposits by checks drawn on another bank and bearing low check numbers

3. Four steps you can take to prevent check kiters are: (1) follow normal check-cashing procedures; (2) do not cash checks against uncollected funds; (3) do not deviate from routine ID procedures and (4) report suspicions to your supervisor

4

CASH HANDLING

OUTLINE

Section 1: U.S. Currency

Section 2: Cash Drawer Arrangement

Section 3: Counting Cash

Section 4: Buying and Selling Cash

Section 5: Mutilated, Unfit, and Counterfeit Money

Section 6: Opening and Closing Procedures

OBJECTIVES

When you have completed this module, you will be able to

- Explain the use of different cash compartments
- Demonstrate how to count cash efficiently
- Describe how to recognize mutilated, unfit, altered, and counterfeit money
- Identify teller opening and closing procedures

INTRODUCTION

Many of the transactions you handle during the day will involve cash. In *Cash Handling*, you will learn why it is important to

- Be familiar with the features of U.S. currency
- Arrange your cash drawer in a specific and consistent way
- Know how to count cash correctly

You will also learn how to recognize altered and counterfeit money, which will help protect your bank from losses. This course also provides you with guidelines for handling mutilated and unfit currency.

In addition, you will learn about teller opening and closing procedures, which include verifying your cash on hand at the start and end of the workday.

SECTION 1: U.S. CURRENCY

The printing of U.S. currency falls under the responsibility of the Federal Reserve System of the United States (see appendix C). From the type of paper that is used to the timing and amount to be printed, the process is closely monitored and highly regulated. In this section, you will learn why it is important for you to know as much as you can about the money you will be working with every day.

Since 1929, one side of each denomination has been printed with the portrait of a specific famous American. On the other side, you will find images that represent national buildings with some historic significance. The exception to the building images is the one dollar bill, where you will find instead the Great Seal of the United States.

Here is a listing of the portraits you will find on what is commonly referred to as the front or face of each denomination.

Denomination	Portrait
$1	George Washington
2	Thomas Jefferson
5	Abraham Lincoln
10	Alexander Hamilton
20	Andrew Jackson
50	Ulysses S. Grant
100	Benjamin Franklin

In addition to the portrait, the face of the bill contains certain key elements. The image below illustrates a few of the elements commonly found on the face of bills. These elements include the denomination, Federal Reserve Bank seal, serial number, and Treasury Department seal.

Take a one dollar bill out of your wallet to become more familiar with its elements. Notice the following parts of the bill as you handle it:

Paper
Red and blue fibers are embedded in the paper.

The Federal Reserve Bank seal
The Federal Reserve Bank seal appears to the left of the portrait.

Value amount
- The value amount of each bill is in all four corners on both sides
- The value is spelled out across the bottom of the face side

District number

The number of the Federal Reserve district that issued the bill appears near all four corners on the face of the bill.

The Treasury seal

Treasury seal appears to the right of the portrait, embossed over the dollar amount.

Serial number

- The unique serial number of the bill appears in both the lower left and the upper right of the face of the bill
- The first letter of the serial number is the same as the letter inside the Federal Reserve Bank seal

Exhibit 4-1 Face of the Denomination

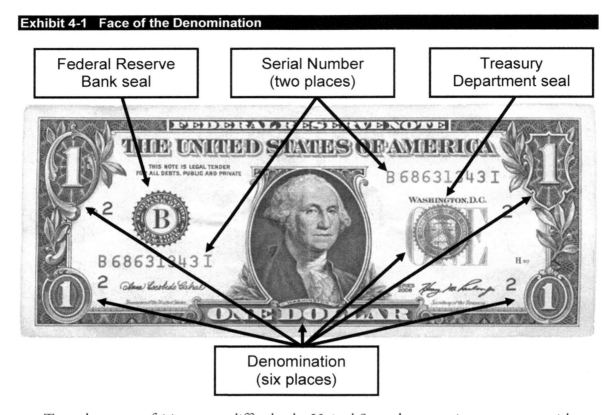

Federal Reserve Bank seal

Serial Number (two places)

Treasury Department seal

Denomination (six places)

To make counterfeiting more difficult, the United States began to issue currency with additional security features in 1996. The most common bills—the $100, $50, $20, $10, and $5 are all in circulation with the enhanced security features. The latest security enhancements can be seen in the $100 note that was placed into circulation in 2013.

Below are the differences you will find in the new bills issued after 1996. Notice that the placement of the new security features varies slightly for each denomination.

Watermark. Each denomination has a watermark that appears to the right of the portrait on the face of the bill. The watermark duplicates the portrait shown on that denomination. You can see the watermark by holding the bill up to the light. The same watermark can also be seen on the back of the bill.

Security thread. A thread is embedded into the face of the bill. This thread runs vertically through the bill and can be seen on either side of the bill by holding it up to the light. On the thread are printed "USA" and the denomination amount. When held under an ultraviolet light the thread will glow a different color for each denomination ($100: red; $50: yellow; $20: green; $10: orange; $5: blue).

Fine line printing patterns. Fine line printing appears behind the portraits on the face of the bill and the images on the back side of the bill. These fine lines are extremely difficult to replicate.

Microprinting. The amount of the denomination and "United States of America" are both spelled out on the bill.

Color-shifting ink. In the lower right corner on the face of the bill you will see a large number that matches the value of the bill. When you look at the bill held directly in front of you, this number appears green. But when you hold the bill at an angle, the number appears black. (Note: The $5 bill does not have this color-shifting ink.)

Low-vision feature. The large numeral in the lower right corner on the back of the bill is designed for individuals who may be in poor-visibility locations or have impaired vision. This feature also contains a machine-readable feature that will allow people who are blind to use a scanning device to identify the denomination of the bill.

Beginning with a new $20 note issued in October, 2003, two additional security features have been added.

- *Symbols of freedom.* Symbols of freedom representing icons of Americana are now part of the design. Two images are printed on the face of the note, one in the background to the left of the portrait, the other on the lower right side of the portrait. The symbols of freedom differ for each denomination. For $10 notes, an image of the torch carried by the Statue of Liberty and the words "We the People" are used; on $20 notes, images of eagles appear; on $50 notes, parts of the American flag.
- *Subtle background colors.* These colors, different for each denomination, are intended to help everyone, especially those who are visually impaired, to tell denominations apart and also to make it more difficult for counterfeiters to succeed. To date, the colors are:
  - $5 note: light purple and gray
  - $10 note: orange, yellow, and red
  - $20 note: green, peach, and blue
  - $50 note: blue and red

Because many of the transactions you will handle each day involve cash, it is important to become familiar with the new security features of U.S. currency as new bills are introduced.

The following section will provide an overview of the key security features of common currency denominations. For a detailed description of key security features, visit https://www.uscurrency.gov/.

$100 Bill

The redesigned $100 note was first issued in 2013. The redesigned bill includes two new features, a 3-D security ribbon and a color-shifting Bell in the Inkwell. Additional security features to check: a security thread, a portrait watermark of Benjamin Franklin that is visible from both sides of the note when held to light, color-shifting numeral 100, raised printing, a gold 100, and microprinting.

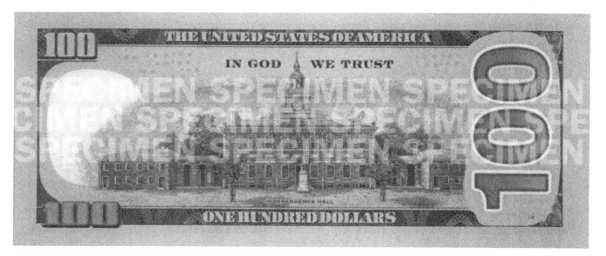

$50 Bill

The redesigned $50 note was first issued in 2004. It has three key security features that are easy to check: a security thread, portrait watermark of Ulysses S. Grant, and color-shifting numeral 50.

$20 Bill

The redesigned $20 note was first issued in 2003. It has three key security features that are easy to check: a security thread, portrait watermark, and color-shifting numeral 20.

$10 Bill

The redesigned $10 note was first issued in 2006. It has three key security features that are easy to check: a security thread, portrait watermark, and color-shifting numeral 10.

$5 Bill

The redesigned $5 note was first issued in 2008. It has three key security features that are easy to check: a column of three small numeral 5 watermarks, a security thread, and a large numeral 5 watermark.

SECTION 2: CASH DRAWER ARRANGEMENT

Just as important as knowing what to look for on a bill is understanding how your cash should be stored throughout your work day. It is not safe to keep all of your cash in one drawer. Although banks may vary on how and where tellers are to store cash, they all are usually consistent on at least three separate compartments.

Many terms are used to describe these three separate cash locations. Check with your supervisor to learn the terms used in your bank. For the purposes of this course, the following terms are used to describe the typical three cash storage areas:

- Working cash drawer

- Working cash vault
- Coin vault

Working Cash Drawer

This is where the cash you will be accessing most frequently throughout the day is stored. The working cash drawer is divided into separate compartments for the different denominations. Tellers always keep the same denominations in the same compartment, a technique to prevent accidentally giving a customer the wrong amount of money.

The working cash drawer may contain a separate tray for coins. Coins may also be kept on the counter in a coin dispenser, depending on which type of setup your bank uses. The coin dispenser contains loose coins for normal transactions; there is a slot for each type of coin.

Bait money—currency whose serial numbers have been recorded and stored—is also kept in the top cash drawer. Bait money is handed out only in the event of robbery. Bait money assists law enforcement authorities in tracking and convicting robbers. Your bank may also use dye packs, which are also only handed out in the event of a robbery.

In addition, your working cash drawer may contain an alarm for use during a holdup. Be careful not to trigger this alarm accidentally.

Note: Each bank has its own regulations for cash drawer setup. The image shows an example of how a working cash drawer can be arranged. Check with your supervisor about the cash drawer setup and bait money location.

Working Cash Vault

This is where you store excess cash that exceeds the working cash drawer limit. A teller's working cash vault or cash reserve is often kept below the working cash drawer. This cash vault is frequently used to store large bills ($100s and $50s) as well as any cash waiting to be sold to the bank vault or vault teller and all strapped money. You will be required to store the working cash drawer and the contents of this working cash vault in the bank's vault overnight.

Coin Vault

You will more than likely have a supply of wrapped coin. This coin may be kept in your working cash vault or you may have a separate compartment that can be secured at the teller window overnight.

All of your currency and loose coin must be securely stored and locked before you leave work each day.

Note: Ask your supervisor about your bank's procedures for storing excess cash.

SECTION 3: COUNTING CASH

Technology is affecting the teller's job, including counting cash. Many banks now have machines that count currency and coins. Nevertheless, knowing how to count cash is important if for no other reason than as a backup in case the counting machine breaks down.

Exhibit 4-2   Example of a Working Cash Drawer Arrangement

Bill alarm and bait money	100s	50s	Mutilated bills	Pennies
				Nickels
20s	10s	5s	1s	Dimes
				Quarters

Counting Coins

Coins are packaged in coin wrappers, or rolls, to ensure accurate handling. Coin wrappers have a value printed on the wrappers.

Coin	Number of coins per wrapper	Value of full wrapper
$ .01	50	$ .50
.05	40	2.00
.10	50	5.00
.25	40	10.00
.50	20	10.00
1.00 Eisenhower*	20	20.00
1.00 Susan B. Anthony*	25	25.00
1.00 Sacagawea golden dollar	25	25.00
1.00 Presidential dollar	25	25.00

*Although the Eisenhower and Susan B. Anthony coins are no longer being issued, you may see them occasionally.

To count coins before putting them in rolls, place the coins on a flat surface and count as you slide them in pairs along the surface and over the edge into your hand. If there are enough to make a roll, do so. Then initial, teller-stamp, and date the roll (if required by your bank).

When you open a wrapper of coins, always empty the whole package and verify its contents before putting the coins in the coin drawer or coin dispenser. Because of time and customer service restraints, some banks no longer ask tellers to do this for coin, so ask your supervisor about your bank's policy.

Some banks ask customers who bring in rolls of coins to write their name and account number on the outside of each roll. The number is used to debit the customer's account if the roll has too few coins (short), or to credit the customer's account if the roll has too many coins in the roll (long). However, if you do require customer account numbers on the roll, be sure to mark out the number before giving the roll to another customer. Furthermore, some banks do not accept rolled coins from noncustomers because there is no recourse to recover the funds if the coin rolls contain less money than is represented on the outside of the wrapper.

Counting Currency

There are two primary ways of counting currency, the hand-to-table method and the walk-through method. Each method ensures that no bill is double-counted. Whichever method you use, recount the money as many times as necessary to come up with the same total twice. This means you will always count a stack of currency at least two times.

Because you are a new teller, you may feel a little awkward and slow as you learn to use the preferred counting method of your bank—this is normal. Speed in counting at this stage in your career is secondary to accuracy. Take your time counting and know that your speed will increase with practice.

First, we will review the hand-to-table method. You will learn about the walk-through method later in this section.

Hand-to-Table Method

The hand-to-table method involves counting cash that is in your hands as you place it bill-by-bill onto a counter or table. This method allows you to see the entire bill and provides protection against counterfeit currency, altered currency, and mutilated bills slipping through. You are also less likely to skip a bill using this method, because you will see and touch each bill—ensuring that bills are not stuck together. The customer will also see you counting—reducing the possibility of error or misunderstanding.

Altered currency

It is possible for someone to receive more cash than a piece of currency is worth. How? A person might alter currency or "raise" a genuine bill by tearing off one or two ends or the corners of a smaller denomination bill, such as a 1 or a 5, and replacing them with the ends or corners of a large bill such as a 10, 20, or even a 50.

Exhibit 4-3 shows two ends from a $20 bill that have been pasted onto a $1 bill. The original $20 bill is redeemed for full value as mutilated money, and the "raised" bill is stuck into a package of $20 bills, thereby netting the swindler $19.

Important: This is why it is important for you to learn to *count currency by looking at the portraits*.

Exhibit 4-3   A "Raised" Bill

Note the inconsistencies on the corners of the bill, denoting a "raised" bill.

Example of how a swindler profits from raised bills

A customer requests that a package of $10 bills, worth $1,000, be replaced with two packages of $5 bills, also worth $1,000. She presents her account number and looks familiar. You are rushed, so you decide to count the money by the walk-through method without first unbanding the stack. You count 100 $10 bills and give the customer two packages of $5 bills.

When you unstrap the money later, you find that all but ten of the bills have the numeric "$10" in the corner but a picture of George Washington on them (which you now know is the portrait on $1 bills). The corners of these bills were glued on. The account number turns out to be false, and the bank takes a loss of $900 ($1000 minus $100 in ones.)

To guard against this type of swindle, never count strapped money presented by a customer while it is strapped. It is probably a good idea to use a cash counter machine or the hand-to-table method of counting. If a bill appears altered, check to see if all the corners match the appropriate picture.

Hand-to-table method: unit technique

When using the hand-to-table method, there are several techniques for counting currency. Adopt one and use it consistently. Be certain that the technique you adopt is acceptable at your bank. One example is the "unit technique."

For 5s. Count 5s by saying, "and," "one," "and," "two," "and," "three," "and," "four" and placing a $5 bill down with each word you say. Add a zero to each number you say, and you have your total. For example, if your count ends on "four," the total count is $40; if a count ends on the "and" after "seven," the total is $75.

$5	$10	$15	$20	$25
and	1	and	2	and

For 10s. Count 10s as if they were 1s; then add a zero to the total.

$10	$20	$30	$40	$50
1	2	3	4	5

For 20s. Count 20s as "two, four, six, eight," and so on; add a zero to the total.

$20	$40	$60	$80	$100
2	4	6	8	10

For stacks of 20s. Count out piles of five 20s each ($100 per pile). Count any remaining bills "twenty, forty, sixty," and so on.

Note: Regardless of the technique used, always sort the currency so that all bills of the same denomination are together and check that all of the bills are face up and facing in the same direction.

Walk-Through Method

The walk-through method is often used to count prepackaged money received from the vault.

Caution: Never use this method to count money received from a customer. When using the walk-through method to count money, you only see the corner of the bill, not the portrait, which makes it easy to overlook raised bills.

The walk-through method consists of the following steps:

Step 1: Place the stack of bills on the table or counter.

Step 2: With the thumb and forefinger of one hand, lift back the corner of each bill. Then hold back the counted bills.

Step 3: Check the denomination of each bill as you count.

Step 4: Count the pile twice.

Step 5: If your totals do not agree, repeat the count until they do.

Receiving Currency and Coins

Count all currency and coins in the presence of the customer. The following steps are necessary for receiving currency and coins:

Step 1: Make certain that all currency and coins from the last transaction have been put away before starting a new transaction.

Step 2: Politely excuse yourself from talking with anyone during your counting.

Step 3: Separate the currency from the coins.

Step 4: Count the currency before the coins, following the methods and techniques previously suggested or the ones stipulated by your bank.

Step 5: If any discrepancies exist between your total and the customer's total, count the money again. If a discrepancy still exists, ask the customer to count the money. If totals continue to differ, ask for assistance from your supervisor without leaving the window.

Step 6: Verify the grand total with the amount listed on the deposit slip or other paperwork.

Step 7: Once the totals match, put all the currency and coin into your cash drawer.

Important: *Never* put cash away or remove it from the sight of the person who gave it to you until you have verified that what you received is what is showing on the paperwork. Once the cash is verified, put away all currency or coins before beginning another transaction.

Finding errors

Occasionally you may find your cash drawer out of balance. You will need to learn your bank's policy regarding out-of-balance cash drawers. Some banks do not want tellers spending time looking for differences under certain small amounts, others do. Below are some things you can do before enlisting the assistance of your supervisor in balancing your cash drawer.

- **Recount** your cash

TIP: If the difference is an even amount, say $5.00, begin your cash recount by counting your five-dollar bills. If the difference is $10.00, begin by recounting your ten-dollar bills or your wrapped/rolled dimes.

- Look all around your area for money; under the key board, in the trash, etc.
- Ask someone else to recount your money
- Clear the totals for each denomination and recount and re-enter the values
- Look through your electronic journal and the documents for your transactions
- Count/balance your drawer every few hours, so that you only need to review transactions since the last time you balanced, rather than for your entire shift

Cash Drawer Security

You are responsible for your own cash drawer. Use the following procedures and precautions to protect yourself and your bank:

- Lock all cash and coins in the safe or in the cash drawer, except when in use
- Never leave your cash drawer unattended
- Never let anyone else touch your cash drawer, except under your direct supervision

SECTION 4: BUYING AND SELLING CASH

The amount of cash you need on a particular day depends on the day's activities. Certain banking days require larger amounts of cash than others. For example, you may need extra currency on days when the federal government makes social security payments—around the 3rd of the month—and on paydays of large businesses located near your bank or branch. You might have an unusual number of customers requesting large amounts of cash, requiring you to buy cash from the vault to continue working.

You will have to buy cash to

- Supplement your cash before opening your window
- Supplement your cash during the day if you pay out a large amount of cash
- Obtain money from the vault when you need certain denominations of currency or coins to complete transactions

A cash-in/buy cash ticket is used to record cash added to your cash supply. A cash-out/sell cash ticket is used to record cash taken out of your cash supply. Many banks use virtual cash tickets, but some banks continue to use physical tickets.

Some banks require tellers to teller stamp the cash sold to the vault during the day. This process identifies the funds as belonging to a particular teller so that discrepancies can be traced back to the teller selling the cash. This procedure may become particularly important if your teller drawer does not balance at the end of the day.

Strapping and Verifying Currency

Currency is strapped to help bank employees count currency quickly. When money is taken out of or put into the vault, the currency generally is bundled or strapped together in specified amounts. Your bank may allow fewer bills to be bundled in partial straps.

Whatever system your bank uses, packages should be initialed and date-stamped by the person who counted and strapped the money. That means that your teller stamp and date should be on every package or bundle of currency in your cash supply.

Exhibit 4-4   Sample Cash-in and Cash-out Tickets

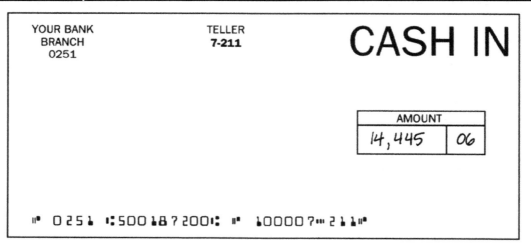

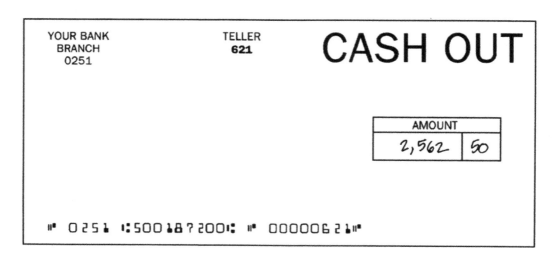

Each package of bills of the same denomination should be strapped with a color-coded or value-imprinted band. Strapped currency is packaged as follows:

Denomination	Number of Bills	Value
$1	100	$100
2	100	200
5	100	500
10	100	1,000
20	100	2,000
50	40	2,000
100	20	2,000

Important: Anytime you encounter a strapped package of money, never assume it contains the proper number of individual bills. Always verify that the strapped package contains the correct currency value by counting the money before putting the cash in your drawer.

SECTION 5: MUTILATED, UNFIT, AND COUNTERFEIT CURRENCY

Mutilated or Unfit Currency

One of your duties as a teller is to remove from circulation all torn, weak, or otherwise damaged money. While the terms "mutilated" and "unfit" are often used interchangeably, the Department of Treasury does distinguish between the two.

Below is how the U.S. Treasury defines these two terms.

Mutilated currency

A mutilated note—not to be confused with an unfit note—is one that is

- Not clearly more than one-half of the original note
- In such condition that the value is questionable and special examination is required to determine its value

The most common causes of currency mutilation are fire; water; chemicals; explosives; animals, especially rodents; insects; petrifaction; and deterioration from having been buried.

Unfit currency

Consists of notes that are worn, soiled, torn, or damaged in some way but do not meet the definition of mutilated currency. For example, if a note is clearly more than one-half of the original note, it is considered unfit currency, not mutilated.

Mutilated currency   **Unfit currency**

Department of the Treasury

Federal Reserve Banks accept unfit currency that banks have received from their customers, and will replace the unfit currency with new bills. The Federal Reserve Banks do not accept mutilated currency. Some banks will explain to the customer that a mutilated bill must be sent to the Treasury to determine whether it can be honored at face value. The bank will also ask the customer to reduce the cash transaction amount by the claimed face value of the mutilated bill. If the Treasury verifies the face value amount and determines that the bill may be honored, the bank adds the amount to the customer's account.

Other banks have made the decision not to accept mutilated currency. Tellers in these banks are instructed to give the customer the address of the Department of the Treasury where the bill should be sent.

Department of the Treasury
Bureau of Engraving and Printing

MCD/OFM, Room 344A
P.O. Box 37048
Washington, DC 20013

Note: It is suggested that mutilated currency be sent by "Registered Mail, Return Receipt Requested." Insuring the shipment is the responsibility of the sender.

Counterfeit Currency

Identifying Counterfeit Currency

The easiest way to detect counterfeit currency is to compare it with genuine currency. Here are just a few guidelines to help you as you monitor currency for counterfeits.

Genuine	Feature	Counterfeit
Appears lifelike and stands out distinctly from the background. Lines in the portrait are distinct and unbroken.	Portrait	Appears lifeless and flat. Details merge into the background, which is often too dark or mottled. Lines in background are often smudged and broken.
Points are sharp and even all around the seal.	Treasury Seal and Federal Reserve Bank Seal	Points surrounding the seal are uneven and sometimes appear flat.
The fine lines in the border designs of the bill are clear and unbroken.	Border	The lines in the outer margin and scrollwork around the edges of the bill may be blurred and indistinct.
Numbers have distinctive style and are evenly spaced.	Serial Numbers	The numbers may not be uniformly spaced or aligned.
The bill will feel heavy, more like a piece of fabric. Tiny red and blue fibers are embedded throughout the bill. A pin can be used to actually lift these fibers out of the bill.	Paper	The bill will feel smooth, more like the pages in a book. Red and blue lines are printed on the surface of the paper, not embedded into the fiber of the paper.

Handling Counterfeit Currency

Your bank has specific rules for handling counterfeit currency. In general, however, the steps are:

1. Excuse yourself from the customer without indicating a problem
2. Show the bill to the head teller or branch manager
3. If your suspicions are confirmed, write your initials and the date in the white border of the bill
4. You or your supervisor will then explain the situation to your customer
5. Try to determine the circumstances under which your customer received the bill
6. Obtain the customer's name, address, and telephone number. If the customer does not have an account with your bank, try to observe his appearance and, if possible, the license plate number and the make of the car
7. Give the customer a receipt for the bill; list the face amount and the serial number of the bill in question
8. Do not credit the customer's account or substitute a new bill. The customer, not the bank, must accept the loss. If the Treasury Department later determines the bill is legitimate, the customer should then receive credit
9. Complete a written report for the Treasury Department. Both the report and the bill will be given to the Secret Service for further investigation
10. Do not handle the bill more than necessary. Place it in an envelope to prevent adding more fingerprints to it

EXERCISE 4-1 COUNTERFEIT CURRENCY

Your bank has specific procedures for handling counterfeit currency. Write those procedures here, and then answer the following questions.

1. What are the differences between the procedure outlined in this module and your bank's procedure?

2. Mr. Johnson, a new customer, just handed you an obviously counterfeit $50 bill. Following your bank's procedures, what steps should you follow? What specifically would you say to Mr. Johnson?

3. Do you have any concerns about counterfeit currency situations? If so, what are they? Who will you speak to about your concerns?

EXERCISE 4-2 CASH HANDLING AND COUNTING

Refer to your bank's policies to answer the following questions.

1. How should you arrange the bills in your cash drawer? Ask your co-workers or supervisor. Draw a diagram of your cash drawer arrangement below.

2. Do you have bait money? Is your alarm in the cash drawer?

3. Do you have a teller dollar limit for your entire cash supply? Do you have a dollar limit for each compartment in your teller window?

4. Fill in the full and partial strap amounts that are acceptable at your bank:

Denomination	Number of Bills in Strap	Strap Amount
$1		
1		
5		
5		
10		
10		
10		
20		
20		
20		
50		
50		
50		
100		
100		
100		

5. At your bank, whom do you approach when you need to buy or sell cash? What is the procedure for buying or selling cash?

6. What is your bank's policy on replacing mutilated or unfit currency?

7. If you have a customer who is disputing the cash involved in a transaction, which employee will help you? What procedures should you follow to resolve this dispute?

SECTION 6: OPENING AND CLOSING PROCEDURES

Opening Procedures

An important part of cash handling is organization. You should have a standard procedure that you follow daily to ensure consistency in your work habits. Your bank will have a procedure you will need to follow before you open your teller window.

Below are some typical opening procedure steps.

1. Make sure you have the supplies you need, such as coin wrappers and currency straps, blank deposit slips, and so forth
2. Sign on to your teller terminal
3. Notify your supervisor that you are ready to get your cash out of the vault
4. Verify that you have a sufficient supply of cash to start your day

Note: You will learn more about the security issues that are a part of your opening procedures in the *Robbery and Bank Security* module.

Closing Procedures

After you have balanced your cash, you will complete your end-of-the-day responsibilities. Check with your supervisor for the specific procedures your bank follows. Below are some general guidelines.

- Bundle all work
- Secure negotiable items
- Log off your computer
- Lock up all cash
- Search your work area for valuables
- Check the trash to ensure that it contains no sensitive information

Trash should **NEVER** contain any sensitive information. All sensitive information should be placed in the bank's shred bin or shredded by the teller. Sensitive information could include lists of customer names, items containing customer account numbers and balances, and any other personally identifiable financial information. Ask your supervisor about your bank's procedures for shredding sensitive information.

EXERCISE 4-3 OPENING AND CLOSING PROCEDURES

Observe your teller supervisor or another teller, and make a list of everything they do to open or close. Keep the list you create as a resource.

1.

2.

3.

4.

5.

6.

7.

8.

9.

10.

MODULE 4 REVIEW QUIZ

1. Whose portrait appears on a $20 bill?

2. How many nickels are in a roll?

3. How many times must you count currency?

4. What are two advantages of the hand-to-table counting method?

5. What must you do before signing for the money given to you in your cash drawer?

6. Under what circumstances may you leave your cash drawer unlocked and unattended?

7. Why might you want to sell cash?

8. How many $5 bills can you expect to find in a full strap?

9. When can you reimburse a customer for a partial piece of currency?

10. Who accepts the loss for the counterfeit currency identified at your window?

11. Which of the following characteristics indicate a genuine bill?
    - ☐ a. There are red and blue threads passing through the paper.
    - ☐ b. Printing appears shiny.
    - ☐ c. All details and the design are clear and sharp.
    - ☐ d. There is one serial number followed by the letter of the issuing Federal Reserve bank.
    - ☐ e. The Treasury seal has even, saw-toothed points.

12. Which of the following procedures do you follow when handling counterfeit currency?
    - ☐ a. Consult with your supervisor before doing anything.
    - ☐ b. Retain the bill in your possession.
    - ☐ c. Refund the amount of the bill to the customer.
    - ☐ d. Initial and date the counterfeit.
    - ☐ e. Protect the customer's anonymity.
    - ☐ f. Give the customer a receipt for the bill.

5

BANK SECURITY

OUTLINE

Section 1: Robbery

Section 2: Bomb, Kidnapping, and Extortion Threats

Section 3: Opening and Closing Security Procedures

Section 4: Active Aggressor Incidents and Other Emergencies

Section 5: Con Artists and Other Criminals

Section 6: Ethics and Internal Fraud

OBJECTIVES

When you have completed this module, you will be able to

- Demonstrate appropriate behavior before, during, and after a robbery
- Respond to bomb, kidnapping, and extortion threats in a safe manner
- Demonstrate safe daily routines
- Respond to active aggressor incidents and other emergencies in a safe manner
- Recognize potential con artist behavior
- Practice ethical behavior

INTRODUCTION

From the moment you leave your home for the bank, until you step inside your home at the end of the day, security issues should be foremost in your mind. Aspects of security are involved in your daily commute, opening and closing the bank, and serving each customer. Security experts say the best way to handle a difficult situation is to be prepared.

In *Robbery and Bank Security*, you will be provided with the information you need to handle the most common security conditions. The module reviews robbery guidelines, security devices, and bomb, kidnapping, and extortion threats. You will also learn about security related to opening and closing procedures.

In addition, this module includes guidelines for recognizing and foiling con artists. And, you will learn about the personal responsibility of every bank employee to practice ethical behavior.

Your bank will provide additional rules and regulations specific to your location and job responsibilities to help you do your job.

SECTION 1: ROBBERY

Perhaps the most threatening situation possible at a bank is robbery. Robbery must be handled intelligently and calmly by following guidelines learned through proper, consistent, and repeated training. In fact, a federal regulation, Federal Reserve Regulation H, requires banks that are members of the Federal Reserve system to designate a security officer to be responsible for ensuring that all appropriate employees receive regular training about bank robbery. Other agencies, such as the FDIC and the Office of the Comptroller of the Currency (OCC), have instituted similar requirements.

Important: Banks protect people first and assets second.

Categories of Robberies

Robbery is an inherent risk in the financial industry. While every bank works to manage risks where possible, once a robbery has begun, the situation should be handled with appropriate care.

The safety of customers and employees in the branch are the most important priority when a robbery occurs. Employees who are well trained, aware of their surroundings, and who follow established robbery guidelines can help to ensure that a situation remains as safe as possible.

Below are some general categories of robberies.

Morning glory: Robber surprises employee(s) to gain access to the vault or cash before the branch opens for business.

Note and/or verbal demand: Robber privately demands cash either verbally or by passing a note to the teller.

Take over: Robber(s) publicly announce demands and may use force to control the branch.

Important: It is imperative that branch employees thoroughly understand their responsibilities before, during, and after a robbery.

Procedures to Counteract Robbery Attempts

Your actions in a robbery should always be focused on your safety and the safety of those around you.

This section covers some general guidelines to follow in the event of a robbery. Your bank will clearly outline for you its procedures for minimizing the danger of robbery.

Review robbery procedures often. This will help you react calmly if you should experience a robbery.

Secure Your Cash Drawer

Use the following procedures:

- **All cash items should be locked up** when not in use
- **Never allow unauthorized persons** in the teller area
- **Never allow another employee** to use your teller drawer
- **Never leave cash items or other confidential items on the counter** when you must leave your station. The temptation may be too great for someone to steal the cash items or use the confidential information to gain illegal access to another customer's account

Important: Do not keep excessive cash in your cash drawer. All banks limit the amount of cash that may be kept in the cash drawer. Know your cash supply limits.

Use Security Devices

Your bank may use one or more of the following security devices:

- Cameras
- Digital video recorders (DVRs)
- A silent alarm, triggered when you remove a certain bill or stack of bills from your drawer or when a button is pressed
- A "suspicion button" that activates surveillance cameras and alerts the branch manager whenever you suspect an individual is "casing" the bank
- Dye packs that look like a strapped pack of bills and are activated by sensors at bank exits, releasing dye or tear gas after the robber leaves the bank
- Door markers at exits to help you determine the height of the robber
- A holdup description sheet
- Guards or off-duty police officers
- Dated bait money. A record of the serial numbers is stored in the auditing department under vault control. Bait money should be placed so that it can be given to the robber easily and inconspicuously with other money in your cash drawer
- Bait money with GPS to track the robber

Stay Alert

Security experts agree that the best way to prevent robbery is to discourage potential thieves.

- **Be aware of suspicious persons loitering in your bank.** They may be observing the location. Customer service skills can be beneficial in discouraging robbery attempts. By "meeting and greeting" unknown customers within 30 seconds of their entrance, you impress new clients with your prompt customer service. And, you also let a potential robber know he has been "seen" by someone in the bank

- **Notice the behavior of persons who enter your bank minutes before closing.** They may be waiting for other customers to leave so that they can have a captive audience and a leisurely closing-time robbery. Pay attention to how they are watching the movement and actions of others in the building and to the amount of time and attention they are giving to completing forms at a check writing stand
- Some banks post signs instructing customers that hats, masks, and firearms are not permitted on bank premises. If your bank posts this policy, **beware of anyone who does not abide by it and call this to your manager's attention,** but be sensitive to customers who may be wearing head coverings due to physical conditions or for religious reasons

What to Do During a Robbery

Follow these guidelines if you become involved in a robbery:

- **Remain calm.** You want the robber to mirror your behavior. If a nervous person is committing the robbery, do not upset or antagonize the robber. The calmer you are, the calmer the robber will be
- **Do exactly as the robber asks.** Assume the robber is armed even if you do not see a weapon
- **Do not be a hero.** You may put yourself and those around you in greater danger by trying to apprehend the robber or refusing his or her request. Your primary goal at this point is to do what the robber asks so that he or she will leave the building as quickly as possible
- **Give the robber exactly what he or she asks for.** For example, if the robber asks for your 20s and 10s, then that is all you should give. Do not copy the actions of one teller who, when a robber asked for all her 20s and 10s, responded by asking "Don't you want my 50s and 100s too?"
- **Try to give small denominations**
- **Activate the silent alarm,** but only when it is safe to do so. Keep in mind that this may be safe to do only after the robber has exited the bank
- **Include the bait money and dye pack** if it seems safe to do so
- **Remember the distinguishing features of the robber.** You will be asked to describe the robber by completing your bank's suspect profile or holdup description form
- **Watch over all evidence left by the robber.** If a note was used in the robbery, keep it in a guarded spot safe from additional fingerprints. If an envelope is handy, you can use the top of your finger or the eraser end of a pencil to slide the note into the envelope to save for law enforcement officials
- **Remember everything the robber touches**
- **Listen to what the robber says** as well as to voice inflections and slang. This information may be helpful in identifying and apprehending the robber

Remember the distinguishing features of the robber

This is not an easy task. Many individuals involved in a robbery that involves a firearm can provide law enforcement with a detailed description of the firearm but not the robber.

Example

Police: Can you describe the robber?

Teller: Umm… white, I think. Or maybe Hispanic, possibly black. About 5'6" or could have been 6'5", I'm not sure. I think he was wearing a hoodie and was clean shaven or he might have had a beard. He might have been bald, but could have had a full head of hair. Hair was black or blond. Maybe brown. He weighed around 165 or it could have been 265. He was a big guy. Sorry, I'm just not sure.

Police: Did the robber have a firearm?

Teller: It was a 45-caliber black metal with a white handle, semi-automatic with a laser sight and had the serial number shaved off.

Review the information on the Robbery Description form carefully (exhibit 5-1). This form is from the ABA Bank Robbery Deterrence Toolbox. These are the kinds of details you should observe during the course of a robbery. Your observation skills will improve with practice. You can practice by observing people or pictures of people in a magazine, and then trying to fill out these forms from memory.

Exhibit 5-1   Robbery Description Form

Tool 3   ABA Bank Robbery Deterrence Toolbox

Robbery Description Form

Fill in the blanks immediately after a robbery and before you compare notes with anyone else. Describe or circle only those items you are sure of. Use the blank figure to draw in hard-to-describe details such as patterns of clothing and/or location of scars. Please provide additional copies of this form for each robber.

Date of Robbery:			Time:		
Institution or Company Name:					
Branch:					
Address:					
Phone:					
Your Name:					
Home Address:					
Phone:					
Email Address:					
Position:					
Signature:					
Date:			Time:		
SPEECH:	Loud Refined Other: (describe):	Soft Rapid	Lisp Nasal	Slow Deep	High-Pitched Stutter
ACCENT:	Local Other (describe):	Eastern	Southern	Western	Foreign
WEAPON:	Semiautomatic Pistol Automatic Rifle COLOR:	Revolver Submachine Gun Black	Knife Shotgun Shiny	Rifle Sawed-Off Shotgun Other:	
DESCRIBE WEAPON					
ROBBERY DETAIL	Did robber use a note? Yes No Did you retain note? Yes No				
	If you were unable to keep the note – what did it say?				
	If robber spoke – what did he or she say?				
	Did the robber have an accomplice you were aware of? Yes No				

3-10   © 2015 AMERICAN **BANKERS** ASSOCIATION, Washington, D.C.

ABA course content does not provide, nor is it intended to substitute for, professional legal advice.

Exhibit 5-1 continued

ABA Bank Robbery Deterrence Toolbox   Tool 3

ROBBER'S ESCAPE	Don't Know On Foot Car Other Vehicle Type of Vehicle:
ESCAPE VEHICLE	Make:
	Model:
	Color:
	Year:
	License Number:
	Number of Other Passengers in Vehicle:
	Direction Taken:
ADDITIONAL NOTES OR DESCRIPTIONS	

Exhibit 5-1   continued

Tool 3   ABA Bank Robbery Deterrence Toolbox

HEIGHT:	WEIGHT:		RACE:	APPARENT AGE:
SEX:	Male		Female	
COMPLEXION:	Sallow Ligh Ruddy Freckle Dark			
HAIR COLOR:	Blond Red Brow Gray Blac Partially Gray Other:			
FACIAL HAIR	Beard	Unshaven	Moustache	
HAIR STYLE:	Long Short Medium Bald Wig Straight Medium Curly Partially			
EYEBROWS:	Bushy Thin High Over Eyes Low Over			
EYES:	Large Wide Set Small Close Together Pouches Deep Set Droopy			
EYE COLOR:	Blue Gray Hazel Brown Black			
NOSE:	Small Large Long Short Thin Wide			
TEETH:	Straight Crooked Buck Discolore Some Missing			
CHIN:	Long Square Receding Prominent			
EARS:	Small	Prominent		
MASK:	Yes	No		
HANDS:	Right-handed		Left-handed	

Please use the blank figure to draw in any hard-to-describe details such as patterns of clothing or location of scars.

CLOTHING: Circle items and describe:	Suit:	Gloves:
	Jacket:	Hat:
	Sweater:	Shoes:
	Slacks:	Overcoat:
	Skirt or Dress:	Raincoat:
	Tie:	Windbreaker:
	Belt Buckle:	

Other Marks and Characteristics: Describe any disguises or other personal characteristics such as scars, tattoos, birthmarks, limp, twitch, deformities, amputations, or any jewelry such as a watch, ring, necklace, earring, etc., that the robber wore:

_____

_____

_____

_____

_____

Exhibit 5-2 Sample Holdup Description Form

HOLDUP DESCRIPTION FORM

OFFiCE _____   TIME: _____

LOCATION _____   DATE _____

Circle or Check One

SEX . . . . MALE   FEMALE

RACE . . . . WHITE   BLACK   OTHER _____

AGE 15   20   25   30   35   40   45   50   55   Over 55

HEIGHT . . . . Under 5'   5'   5'5'   5'6'   5'7'   5'8'   5'9'   5'10'   5'11'   6'   Over 6'

WEIGHT . . . . Under 120 120 130 140 150 160 170 180 190 200 Over 200

HAIR . . . . Black   Blond   Grey   Red   Brown

Long   Short   Brush   Afro

(Wig) _____

BUILD . . . . Small   Medium   Large   Obese

COMPLEXION . . . . . Light   Medium   Dark

Clear   Ruddy   Other _____

EYES. . . . . Blue   Brown   Hazel   Green

NOSE . . . . Large   Small   Broad   Pug

GLASSES . . . . No _____   Yes _____   If Yes _____

MUSTACHE . . . . No _____   Yes _____   If Yes _____

SIDEBURNS . . . . Long   Short   Thick   Thin

GOATEE . . . . No _____   Yes _____   If Yes _____

BEARD . . . . No _____   Yes _____   If Yes _____

GUN . . . . Automatic   Revolver   S/Shotgun   Other _____

CAR USED . . . . No _____   Yes _____   Make & Year _____

Color _____   Plate No _____

HAT . . . . No _____   Yes _____   COAT . . . . No _____ Yes _____

SHIRT . . . . _____   ACCESSORIES _____

PANTS . . . . _____   SHOES _____

METHOD AND DIRECTION OF ESCAPE _____

_____

DISGUISE AND ADDITIONAL COMMENTS _____

_____

_____

_____

CHECK ONE

(   ) Victim Teller: Name _____

(   ) Witness: Address _____

(   ) Customer: Phone No _____

_____
SIGNATURE

What to Do After a Robbery

Many things will happen once the word of what has occurred reaches other bank employees and customers. Everything will run smoothly as long as you know which personnel will take certain actions if a robbery occurs. Talk with your supervisor about procedures that outline which employee will lock the doors, who will call the police, who will care for the injured, who will look for the getaway car, who will protect the evidence, etc. These procedures should be in place at your branch.

Your primary responsibilities after a robbery are to take the following actions:

- Remain calm
- If you have not yet done so, activate the silent alarm
- Alert closest co-worker to lock the doors
- Write down immediately any information you have been able to observe safely, such as the make and model of the getaway vehicle, the direction the robber ran, the type of clothing the robber wore, and so forth. DO NOT follow the robber out of the building to get such information
- Close your teller window and lock up your cash supply
- Avoid touching your teller area and forbid anyone else to enter your area. Many banks have robbery kits that contain a plastic or paper sheet that can be spread over the teller area to preserve all fingerprints for the law enforcement officials. The morning newspaper can accomplish the same results when spread out over the teller area
- Notify a security officer or other person designated by your bank as soon as it is safe to do so. If you must leave your area for this purpose, be sure to secure your cash before leaving
- Do not discuss details of the robbery with anyone, including other employees, until you have had a chance to write down everything you can remember about the robber and the details of the robbery. Details tend to get distorted when told repeatedly
- Be prepared when asked to balance your cash supply to verify the amount taken in the robbery

Procedures after a robbery

While you are writing down the details of the robbery, other bank employees, such as a branch manager or a security officer, will be taking steps to assist the law enforcement officials and ensure the safety of people remaining in the building. Those steps will include:
1. Locking the doors to the branch.
2. Taking the names and addresses of those who witnessed the robbery.

There is no legal requirement by the Federal Reserve or any other governmental body that a bank's customers are to remain in a bank after a robbery until they are released by the police. When a robbery occurs, bank personnel are supposed to obtain the names and contact information of all customers that were in the bank at the time of the robbery; but bank employees typically are not instructed to keep customers in the bank, have no authority to restrain customers from leaving the bank, and should not attempt to do so.

3. Reminding bank employees that they are not to speak to the media.

4. Monitoring the doors to ensure that only the police and bank officials are allowed into the bank after the robbery.

5. Placing a sign on the door of the branch stating that the branch is closed and directing customers to the nearest branch location.

Additional resources

Documented procedures: Your bank's security officer will have documented the bank's safety procedures. Ask your supervisor where your bank's safety procedures are located (for example, in the bank's Security Manual or Teller Manual). Be sure to follow these steps precisely and thoroughly.

Intranet website: Ask your supervisor about any internal websites that house information and resources such as branch security procedures, employee awareness, bank robber wanted posters, security alerts, and security personnel contact lists.

JOB AID 5-1 WHAT SHOULD I DO IF THE BANK IS ROBBED?

Law enforcement experts agree: if the possibility of robbery exists, be prepared. One way to be prepared and feel confident is to create a job aid that will help you in a robbery and review it frequently.

List your bank's procedures to follow during a robbery. Transfer your answers later to a five- by seven-inch index card and tape it to a visible spot in your teller station.

In the event of a robbery, I should follow these instructions:

1. Remain calm.
3. _____
4. _____
5. _____
6. _____
7. _____
8. _____
9. _____
10. _____
11. _____
12. _____
13. _____

After a robbery, you may be too distraught to remember the many steps necessary to secure the scene. List your bank's procedures to follow after a robbery.

After the robbery, I should take the following steps:

1. Lock the doors.
2. _____
3. _____
4. _____
5. _____
6. _____
7. _____
8. _____
9. _____
10. _____
11. _____
12. _____
13. _____
14. _____
15. _____

SECTION 2: BOMB, KIDNAPPING, AND EXTORTION THREATS

Bank personnel may also encounter other security threats such as bomb, kidnapping, or extortion threats.

Important! Always take bomb, kidnapping, and extortion threats seriously.

Bomb Threats

Criminals create bomb threats to cause an evacuation of the bank so that they can have easy access to funds. You may receive a bomb threat over the telephone, and when you do, you need to be familiar with the specific measures to follow.

Access the link below to review Bomb Threat Call Procedures and Bomb Threat Checklist developed by the Federal Emergency Management Agency (FEMA).

https://emilms.fema.gov/is906/assets/ocso-bomb_threat_samepage-brochure.pdf

Kidnapping Threats

Bank employees could be targets for a kidnapper. A criminal might also call the bank and say that a kidnapping has already occurred. The criminal hopes the bank will pay for the safe return of an employee or the family member of an employee.

Senior bank officials are also exposed to kidnapping threats. As a bank employee, you must keep the location and activities of your senior bank management confidential always. Do not under any circumstances reveal such information to someone who has no need to know, not even to your own family and friends. If a caller seems persistent about obtaining this type of information, refer the call to a supervisor or security officer. You could jeopardize the safety of others at your bank if you violate this rule.

All bank employees are potentially vulnerable to kidnapping threats. Review Job Aid 5-2 to learn about the steps you should follow if a telephone caller threatens to kidnap you or anyone else.

JOB AID 5-2   WHAT SHOULD I DO IN A KIDNAPPING?

Place this list next to your telephone and computer.

- Cooperate with the kidnapper. Be respectful
- Do not play hero
- If you receive a call, try to keep the caller on the phone as long as possible while alerting coworkers. Some banks will have a brightly colored card you can wave in the air to alert other bank staff that you have a bomb threat or kidnapping threat call. The longer you talk with the caller, the more information you may gain. It also may be possible to have the call traced
- If you receive an email, alert your coworkers immediately
- Record the exact time of the call or email and any other details
- Listen carefully to the caller. Be aware of accents, slang, and background noises. Pay close attention to the details in an email
- Notify your supervisor and bank security immediately
- Refer to your bank's procedures regarding kidnapping

Extortion Threats

The term extortion refers to the crime of obtaining money or property by using threats of harm against the victim, or against his property or family.

Extortion is a crime in which one person attempts to force another person to do something against his will. Extortion is most often used in a banking situation to force the bank to give property or money to the perpetrator, or to take some action, such as rehiring someone or stopping an action such as foreclosure or repossession. This is done by threatening the victim's property, person, or loved ones with harm or intimidating the victim.

The primary difference between extortion and robbery is that extortion requires the perpetrator to make a threat verbally, or in writing; robbery does not. Robberies generally offer immediate gratification to the robber, while the extortionist will force the victim to willingly hand over whatever the extortionist is asking for to avoid future repercussions.

Extortion may not always involve a phone call or in-person threat. You may be familiar with the term "ransomware." Cyber-attacks against financial institutions to extort payment in return for the release of sensitive information are increasing. Banks need to be particularly worried about the rise in extortion-related cyberattacks because cyber criminals typically install malware throughout a bank's network making it hard to pinpoint.

Cyber-hackers can get into a bank's website and use the bank's web pages to infect others who use and trust the bank's website. Banks are encouraged to notify law enforcement and their primary regulator or regulators of a cyber-attack involving extortion.

SECTION 3: OPENING AND CLOSING SECURITY PROCEDURES

Personal Safety

Each day, you should follow established safety routines in your commute to and from work and in opening and closing your bank. Review the following tips to ensure your physical security and that of your coworkers.

- Try to vary your morning commute route weekly or even daily. Always taking the same route makes it easy for a criminal to detect your established routine, which could make you an easy target for kidnapping or extortion
- Be observant in case you are being followed. If you suspect that someone is following you, do not go home or to the bank. Go to the nearest police or fire station or to any public place from which you can call the police
- Remember, since you are a bank employee, you are a potential hostage. Stay alert and be proactive and confident. For example, do not look down at your phone when entering the bank—if you are distracted, you are at risk

Opening Procedures

Security officers suggest that employees responsible for opening the branch and the initial search follow the procedures below.

Initial search

The "searcher" should go inside and search the premises while the other one watches from outside. The "searcher" will be checking any areas where someone could hide, such as the bathrooms, closets, beneath open areas such as desks and teller stations, and break rooms.

Predetermined signal

When the search is over, the searcher gives a predetermined signal to the waiting employee that it is safe to enter. If the employee waiting outside does not receive the signal, he or she should contact a security officer or the police.

Opening code signal

To let the later arriving employees know that it is safe to enter, the searcher activates an opening code signal, which may be something like opening a curtain, moving a plant, or turning on the external light in the drive-in window. The opening code signal should be changed frequently to ensure safety. All subsequent arriving employees should be let in the door by employees inside and should not gain access by means of their keys.

Important: If you arrive at the bank and the all-clear signal has not been given, wait outside for the signal or contact the appropriate bank personnel to let them know the building has not been secured. Sometimes the person responsible for securing the premises has just forgotten to give the "all-clear" signal, but never assume that is the case. If the all-clear signal is not displayed, it should always be treated as a dangerous situation.

Your bank will have specific opening security procedures that you need to know.

Work with your supervisor to identify the security procedures you are expected to follow. Document them on this sheet for your reference, until you are able to commit them to memory.

Closing Procedures

Before the bank is vacated at the close of business each day, certain procedures should be completed.

Step 1: Teller area searched for valuables.

Step 2: Look in safe deposit booths and the vault to ensure that all customers and employees have left.

Step 3: Terminals logged off.

Step 4: Bank premises searched for unauthorized persons (supply rooms, restrooms, break rooms, unused offices, and large cabinets).

Step 5: All cash drawers in the vault; vault set and locked.

EXERCISE 5-1 OPENING SECURITY PROCEDURES

Meet with your supervisor and review the following questions:

1. When I arrive at the bank, how do l know it is safe to enter the building?

2. Who is responsible for opening the bank?

3. Is there a special signal I should look for indicating that it is safe to enter?

4. If I suspect there is a problem, what should I do?

SECTION 4: ACTIVE AGGRESSOR INCIDENTS AND OTHER EMERGENCIES

Active Aggressor

An active aggressor is one who has attacked with deadly force one or more persons, and who will continue to randomly seek out and kill as many people as possible. The shootings at Columbine High School, Sandy Hook Elementary School, Ft. Hood Texas, and the Fort Lauderdale airport are examples of active shooter incidents. Active aggressor situations can start as a bank robbery and quickly escalate into this type of occurrence.

Banks should institute an emergency action plan for an active aggressor situation and prepare staff to effectively respond and help minimize loss of life.

It is important for employees to be trained so that they can react if they are ever confronted with an active aggressor situation. As these situations evolve rapidly, quick decisions could mean the difference between life and death. If you are in harm's way, you will need to determine the safest course of action based on the scenario that is unfolding before you. It is likely that your bank has procedures that it wants employees to follow in these types of volatile cases.

Below are some valuable resources on active aggressor situations.

The Department of Homeland Security (DHS) has created an excellent printed training workbook and you can download it for free at http://www.dhs.gov/xlibrary/assets/active_shooter_booklet.pdf.

The Federal Emergency Management Agency (FEMA) has also released an active shooter brochure found at http://www.fema.gov/media-library-data/1472672897352-d28bb197db5389e4ddedcef335d3d867/FEMA_ActiveShooter_OnePagerv1d15_508_FINAL.pdf.

Fire and Emergency Evacuations

In the event of a fire, an emergency evacuation due to an act of nature (tornado, hurricane, flood or even a potential terrorist attack) your first concern should be people's safety—your own, your coworkers', and your customers'. If you have time before leaving your window, place currency, cash, checks, and deposits in your cash drawer and return it to the vault, or lock your drawer. Do not take your cash drawer outside the teller or vault areas. Be sure to follow the fire and evacuation procedures outlined for your building.

Emergency action plan (EAP)

In general, banks should create an emergency action plan (EAP) with input from several stakeholders including the human resources department, training department (if one exists), the bank security officer, local law enforcement and/or emergency responders.

An effective emergency action plan (EAP) includes the following areas:

- A preferred method for reporting fires and other emergencies
- An evacuation policy and procedure
- Emergency escape procedures and route assignments (i.e., floor plans, safe areas)
- Contact information for, and responsibilities of individuals to be contacted under the EAP
- Information concerning local area hospitals (i.e., name, telephone number, and distance from your location)
- An emergency notification system to alert various parties of an emergency including:

  - Individuals at remote locations within the premises
  - Local law enforcement
  - Local area hospitals

General Precautions to Take as Preparations for an Emergency

- Locate the nearest exit
- Rehearse your escape route
- Participate in emergency drills
- Locate and map the locations of all fire extinguishers and safe rooms. (In the case of a tornado or hurricane, if there is no basement, very often a vault or a bathroom is the safest place to be.)

When a Fire or Other Emergency Occurs

- Sound the alarm and notify the fire department, if applicable
- Advise others of the situation
- If the emergency involves a fire, attempt to extinguish the fire if you think you can do so safely. Never use water on an electrical fire
- If an evacuation is necessary, attempt to secure all valuables in the vault as time permits
- Evacuate persons with disabilities
- Evacuate all others. Remember, in case of fire, use stairways, not elevators, to evacuate the building

JOB AID 5-3   WHAT SHOULD I DO IN A FIRE?

In a fire, preparation and rehearsal are the key to staying alive. Complete this job aid on fire safety and keep it in your work area.

- Whom do I call in the event of a fire?

- What is the procedure for evacuating customers and employees safely?

- Where is the nearest fire extinguisher?

- What is the bank's procedure when a fire is discovered in a wastebasket?

- What is the procedure for securing my cash drawer in the event of a fire?

SECTION 5: CON ARTISTS AND OTHER CRIMINALS

New tellers are a favorite target of con artists. Con artists hope that a new teller can be confused and exasperated easily and, therefore, made to hurry through a transaction. They believe that in the confusion a new teller will do something that financially benefits them, something that a teller would not normally do. These criminals particularly look for a teller station without a nameplate, indicating a new teller. Even seasoned tellers have been victims of these cons.

Behavior of the Con Artist

Complain in a loud voice

Con artists may complain in a loud voice so that others will hear

- That you are slow
- You do not know your job

Impress you

Con artists may try to impress you by

- Implying that they are of a higher social class
- Referring to their success in business
- Wearing expensive clothes and jewelry

Distract you

Con artists may distract you by

- Speaking with a shaking voice
- Acting fearful of being discovered
- Flashing a long string of identification that later proves to be stolen, counterfeit, or unacceptable

Gain your cooperation

Con artists may try to gain your cooperation by

- Maintaining a constant flow of chatter
- Talking about subjects unrelated to their bank transaction
- Using your first name in an attempt to create a sense of familiarity
- Being over friendly
- Working in teams to divert your attention

Guidelines for Handling a Suspected Con Artist

- Do not let yourself be hurried or harassed. If the con artist is making you uncomfortable, slow down, ignore the person, and proceed carefully and slowly. If necessary, close your window, secure your drawer and walk away
- Con artists may become violent if you try to apprehend them. Instead, try to refer them to your supervisor

- Check your bank's policy on exchanging currency for noncustomers. Many banks will not permit tellers to exchange currency for noncustomers without a supervisor's approval. The con artist may give you a counterfeit or attempt to confuse you into paying out an incorrect amount by appearing to change his mind about the type of change he needs

Example

The con artist presents a $50 bill and asks you for two $20s and a $10, which you give him. Then he says, "You know what? I think I may need some $5s, so can you give me eight $5s instead?" While you are reaching for the eight $5s the con artist talks to you and distracts you. You discover later that instead of giving you two $20s he gave you one $20 and one $10, giving him an extra $10. This all happens very quickly. Even experienced tellers have been taken in by this technique.

- Tell the suspect that you are not authorized to complete the transaction, then call your supervisor
- If you cannot complete the transaction, use your good customer service skills to offer an alternative
- Accusations can provoke a con artist or offend an honest customer. Remain friendly and polite
- Be prepared to push the "suspicious" button to take a picture (if your bank has this system) or to write down a description if the suspect leaves suddenly. Many banks will encourage you to use the *Robbery Description form* as a prompt for remembering details about the suspected con artist
- If it is safe to get the information, note the make, model, color, and license number of the suspect's car
- If you have not notified someone during the transaction, notify your supervisor as soon as the suspect leaves

Other Criminal Activities

Bank customers also can be victimized by criminals. Banks frequently send brochures to customers reminding them to be alert when using automated teller machines and to safeguard checkbooks and credit cards against pickpockets. Banks also ask their customers to inform them if new checks or bank statements are not received promptly.

There are several scams in which customers can be conned out of large sums of money. If you serve a customer who requests a large sum of cash, always offer the customer an alternative to the cash, such as a cashier's check or traveler's checks. Mention the danger of carrying large amounts of cash. If you feel the situation warrants it, you might even ask a few questions to determine what the customer is using the cash for. If the situation seems unusual, advise your manager before transacting further business. You could be preventing a valued customer from being swindled out of his or her life savings.

Felony Lane Gang

The Felony Lane Gang was a group of individuals who found a way to con banks. The men in the group smashed car windows and searched for ID cards, credit cards, and checkbooks. With those IDs and stolen checks, the gang member went through the drive-thru of a bank, accompanied by a woman gang member who resembled the victim's ID. The gang would cash stolen checks for large sums of money from the victim's account.

The "felony lane" describes the farthest drive-up lane from a bank teller, distant enough to make it harder to identify on surveillance cameras.

Elder Financial Abuse

The elderly are particularly vulnerable to con artists and other criminals. For detailed information on your bank's role and responsibilities in protecting elderly clients, see ABA's Frontline Compliance course *Elder Financial Abuse.*

Scams

Scammers often try to trick people into depositing fake cashier's checks and money orders. At some point, the scammer attempts to persuade the victim to withdraw the excess funds and wire them to pay some sort of fee or taxes.

The key here is that there is often an accompanying request to wire the funds: either the same day as the deposit or a day later. This is where tellers may get involved. If a customer asks when the check will be cleared, the teller should explain to the customer that while funds will be available on a certain date, that does not mean the check is good. The teller should make clear that the check could still be returned and that the customer is responsible for any funds withdrawn.

Also, where appropriate, for example if a customer asks whether a check is "good," the teller should make further inquiries about the source of the check. References by the customer to lotteries, Internet sales, and wiring funds to foreign countries should raise red flags, and the teller should get the attention of a supervisor.

The newspapers often carry stories about people who have been taken in by con artists. These con artists will insist on cash for something like roof repairs, paving a driveway, or insurance policies. Customers who fall for this scam discover too late that the person they gave the cash to was in fact a con artist. If you suspect this might be happening, remind the customer that when any business insists on cash, great caution should be used before continuing the transaction.

SECTION 6: ETHICS AND INTERNAL FRAUD

As a bank employee, you have a personal responsibility to adhere to the ethics and guidelines established by your institution. If you were not given a copy of your bank's code of ethics when you were hired, you should request one and become familiar with the requirements. Employees may be dismissed for violating any of the bank's code of ethics requirements.

The following requirements are commonly found in banks' ethics policies:

Personal banking

- Do not conduct any financial transaction for yourself or a family member through your own teller work. Always have another teller handle your personal banking
- If you need to change your own bill or coin for personal use, ask another teller to change it for you out of his or her cash drawer or personal vault

Holding checks

- Do not substitute other employees' checks for cash and "hold" them in your vault overnight. Never ask other employees to make such transactions for you

Cash drawer security

- Lock your cash drawers and secure your window if you leave the area
- Never allow other employees to have access to your cash. You should be the only one handling the cash in your drawer or personal vault
- Never borrow cash from your cash drawer or vault. Taking any funds from your cash drawer or vault or someone else's is considered embezzlement

Cash drawer balancing

- If your cash is out of balance, you should represent the true figure. Never use personal funds or a secret supply of cash ("kitty") to create the illusion that you are in balance

Information security

- The account information you process at work is confidential. Do not discuss it outside the bank

Important: If you are confused about any of these guidelines, your supervisor can clarify your bank's policy.

MODULE 5 REVIEW QUIZ

1. What three procedures will help you remain vigilant to the possibility of a robbery and counteract it?

2. Should you cooperate with the robber's demand for money? If so, how much should you give?

3. Should you follow the robber out of the bank?

4. Why should you "meet and greet" all unknown customers?

5. List six of the steps your bank recommends that tellers follow during a robbery.

6. Why do criminals usually make bomb threats?

7. What bank personnel are most likely to be the object of a kidnapping or extortion?

8. How can you help protect bank personnel from a kidnapping threat?

9. List at least five procedures a teller should follow when a potential kidnapper calls.

10. You arrive for work at the bank and notice that the opening code signal has not been activated. What should you do?

11. What should be your first concern in an emergency?

12. List at least two specific precautions can you take to be prepared in the event of an emergency.

13. What should you do with your cash drawer during a fire if you have the time?

14. What procedures should you follow during a fire?

15. List four behaviors typical of a con artist.

16. A well-dressed customer arrives at your window and requests to exchange a $500 bill into $20s. While you count out the cash, he loudly complains that you are taking too long, and you should hurry with the transaction as he is very busy and pressed for time. Which action below should you take?

    a. Complete the transaction in a hurry to show good customer service, and send the customer on his way
    b. Tell the customer that you cannot complete the transaction in his timeframe, and then call your supervisor
    c. Tell the customer that you will not conduct this type of service for him in the future

17. What should you do if a confused, hurried customer attempts to withdraw $5,000 cash or if a customer who normally withdraws only $1,000 a month wants to withdraw $5,000?

18. At the close of the day, you are 37 cents short. You take the change from your wallet and indicate that your cash vault balances. Is this proper procedure?

6

PROVIDING QUALITY CUSTOMER SERVICE

OUTLINE

Section 1: Customer Expectations

Section 2: Communication Skills

Section 3: Dealing with All Kinds of Customers

Section 4: Product Knowledge Skills

Section 5: Helping Customers Understand the Rules

OBJECTIVES

When you have completed this module, you will be able to

- Respond to various expectations customers bring to the bank
- Demonstrate effective communication skills
- Manage difficult customers professionally
- Use information about your bank's specific products and services to help customers
- Help customers understand banking rules

INTRODUCTION

In recent years, many changes have occurred in the banking industry. You may have noticed an increase in the number of products and services your own bank offers. But more importantly, have you noticed a difference in the way you are treated when you visit a bank? Banks, along with all other businesses in the service industry, have learned just how important providing quality customer service can be. From the doctor's office to the grocery store, businesses know that their customers could have chosen a competitor. Banks continuously strive to increase the quality of service to retain and satisfy their customers.

In *Providing Quality Customer Service*, you will learn how to go beyond the level of service customers have come to expect. You will have an opportunity to sharpen your communication abilities and enhance your skills to serve a variety of customers. You will also develop your knowledge of general banking products—a key element in providing quality customer service.

SECTION 1: CUSTOMER EXPECTATIONS

Successful businesses place the treatment of their customers high on their priority list. Customers who feel valued, return with more business and refer new customers. These word-of-mouth referrals are a very inexpensive, yet are an extremely effective way of advertising.

Customers who do not feel valued, do not return, and they share their unpleasant experiences with several people who might have been customers before they heard about these experiences.

A bank's profits rise when its number of customers increases. Profits grow dramatically when existing customers increase the business they give to the bank by opening new accounts or by investing more money in their present accounts. Quality service causes both the number of customers and the value of accounts to increase. You can contribute to the increase in customer accounts by consistently going beyond what your customers expect from you as you interact with them in your daily routine.

Quality service has three major components: commitment; customer satisfaction; and efficient, error-free service.

- *Commitment.* For the teller, total commitment means wanting to do the best job possible for the bank and its customers. Your goal as a teller is to serve the customers in a manner that builds on the trusting relationship between banker and customer.
- *Customer satisfaction.* Customer satisfaction is the degree to which a customer's expectations are met or exceeded. Everything done in a bank is ultimately directed at satisfying the needs of customers. Customers expect to learn about new products and services that would be of benefit to them. Many customers have been lost to competing banks because an institution failed to consider its customers' individual needs. You should concentrate your efforts on keeping new and existing customers satisfied.
- *Efficient, error-free service.* You must provide efficient, error-free service. Customers have the right to assume that every transaction involving one of their accounts will be free of error. Their money and personal, confidential information are at stake. Customers cannot be expected to tolerate errors.

The Customer Experience

The overall customer experience is vital to the success of your bank. By consistently applying the components of quality service—commitment, customer satisfaction, and efficient, error-free service—you can help to ensure that customers are giving your bank high marks in the following areas:

- Percentage of customers who would or would not recommend your company
- Customer satisfaction in terms of how well you provide service, recovery, and products for them
- Customer engagement and how well you know or understand your customers' needs

- Customer retention and increased services with you
- How quickly and efficiently you respond or handle their transaction

What Drives Customer Satisfaction?

There is a direct causal relationship between customer experiences in their banking transactions and their level of satisfaction. Satisfied customers are customers who have had their expectations met. Exhibit 6-1 summarizes the causes and effects of customer satisfaction and dissatisfaction.

Exhibit 6-1 further demonstrates a direct link between your behavior with customers and your bank's success. You can and should help create satisfied customers who will increasingly use bank services and encourage others to patronize your bank. It is also within your control to alienate customers and negatively impact the volume of bank business.

Exhibit 6-1   Causes and Results of Customer Satisfaction and Dissatisfaction

	Probable Causes	Likely Results
Satisfied customer	Given a personal and friendly greeting when entering the bank	Will feel appreciated
	Served by a bank employee who completed all transactions in a professional and timely manner	Will have feelings of trust for the bank reinforced
	Used less time than anticipated	Will feel that expectations have been exceeded
	Received useful product/service information	Will consider using additional products/services
	Had problem or issue successfully resolved	Will feel more loyalty for the bank
Dissatisfied customer	Did not achieve all banking goals	Will have a less pleasant day
	Experienced an unanticipated problem	Will make negative remarks to potential customers
	Received bad news about the bank account	May consider switching to another bank
	Experienced an unfavorable impression of bank staff	Will not be eager to use the bank's other services
	Was delayed	Will anticipate problems next time
	Was belittled	Will open accounts at a competitor bank
	Did not receive helpful product information	Will not consider the bank a source of financial information

EXERCISE 6-1 THE SERVICE YOU RECEIVE

The more you practice the behaviors that lead to customer satisfaction, the more you will be able to provide the level of customer service your customers expect and deserve. The following exercise will help you identify customer service behaviors you have experienced, and how they made you feel as a customer.

Recall a recent, very positive experience you had as a customer of a business establishment that provides in-person customer service (perhaps a supermarket, bank, library, doctor's office, or clothing store). On the following chart, identify the type of establishment and describe why the experience was so positive. Consider how the business treated you as a customer. For example, did the employees smile? How did they address you? How did they make you feel? Did they call you by name?

Do the same for a particularly negative experience you have had as a customer. Then answer questions 1 to 5.

Good experience	Bad experience
Type of establishment: The experience:	Type of establishment: The experience

1. Was your good experience positive enough to affect your loyalty to that establishment? Explain.

2. Was your bad experience negative enough to affect your loyalty to that establishment? Explain.

3. What specific employee behavior caused you to feel positively about the experience?

4. What specific employee behavior caused you to feel negatively about the experience?

5. Which positive behavior traits will you commit to using as a teller?

Focus your attention on the answers you provided to questions 3, 4, and 5. Try to understand exactly what actions caused your feelings about the service provided. Placing yourself in your customers' shoes and experiencing these feelings can help you to commit to demonstrating a positive behavior for your customers.

SECTION 2: COMMUNICATION SKILLS

It has been said that eighty percent of the world's problems revolve around the failure to communicate effectively. In banking, effective communication skills are essential in developing a strong customer relationship.

Making the Customer Feel Valued

- *Make greeting customers an action, not a reaction.* Speak as soon as you make eye contact, and try to be the first one to speak. If you know the person's name, use it; for example, "Good morning, Dr. Hopsen." Be sure to smile, no matter how you feel. The teller's window is your stage, and like an actor, you have the job of making people feel appreciated and valued even if you are having an off day.

- *Take notice of the verbal greeting you normally give people.* Consider whether it needs altering for your teller duties. This is not the place for "Howar ya?" "How ya doin'?" "Howzit goin'?" "Wazzup?" or other familiar, colloquial expressions.

  If you say something like, "How are you today?" say it as politely and sincerely as possible, listen for a response, and respond to it. Many people do not really want an answer to their "How are you?" and for some people it has come to be an empty phrase. It is often better to greet with, "It's nice to see you today" and mean it, or simply say, "Hello, Ms. Alvarez," in a tone of voice that says you are glad to see her.

- *Give a business-related compliment now and then.* Personal compliments, no matter how well intended, can have unexpected consequences. "Gosh, you smell good today!" could be perceived as a compliment, but it could also leave the customer wondering how she smelled the other times she visited the bank! However, we all like to hear compliments. In the banking environment, a better choice for complimenting customers might sound like this, "You picked a great time to come in today. We were really busy a little earlier." Or, "This is a great idea to move money from your checking account into your money market so that you can earn a little more interest." Or, "Your deposits are always so organized. Thanks for helping us out like that."

- *Build a professional relationship with your customers that is comfortable for both of you.* Try to remember whatever aspects of their lives they choose to share with you. Keep a mental file of such things as their hobbies, family happenings, career developments, and likes or dislikes so you can show your interest in them later; for example, "How was your trip to Spain, Mrs. Becker?"

  While serving a customer, try to use the customer's name three times—when you greet him or her, while transacting business, and at the close of the transaction. Doing this will help you to remember customers the next time they come in and enable you to add a personal touch to the conversation.

- *Acknowledge the customer's departure with the same enthusiasm you showed in the greeting.* Make eye contact; smile; say, "Goodbye" using the person's name; and thank the customer for coming in. The phrase "Have a nice day" is beginning to acquire a hollow ring, so do not overuse it. Avoid colloquial expressions such as "Have a good one." Some customers may react negatively. Try using such phrases as "Thanks for coming in today," or "See you next week," or something that relates to the conversation you just had; for example, "The next time you come in, please bring a picture of your new granddaughter."

- *Offer an explanation if a transaction or question makes it necessary to leave your work area.* If you need to obtain supervisory approval on a check, or permission to process a transaction that exceeds your authority, explain to the customer at your window why you are leaving. Don't just walk away and leave the customer wondering why. A simple, honest explanation, such as "I need to have my manger sign this check" or "I need to have this approved," is best. Of course, if the issue is possible fraud, you probably don't want to say, "I think this item is fraudulent. Please wait here while I call the police." In a potential fraud situation, say that you need manager approval and let your manager take it from there.

Presenting a Professional Appearance

Communication is more than just the words you speak. While customers expect professionalism in your speech and your behavior, how you and your workplace look also contribute to the image of professionalism you project.

Banking is still considered a conservative environment. Customers are more confident about the bank if the employee to whom they entrust their personal financial transactions presents a conservative and professional image. Pay attention to the elements of that image and take pride in what those elements say about you:

- *Work area.* Keep your counter neat, orderly, and clean. Keep brochures and other materials that customers may request in a convenient and easily accessible area.
- *Dress.* Follow your bank's dress code. Clothes should be clean and pressed and in good taste. Jewelry should not be flashy or excessive. A neat appearance creates a professional image and a better impression on the customer and management. If you question the appropriateness of your attire, chances are it is not appropriate to others.
- *Grooming.* Your hair should be neatly cut and styled. Use makeup tastefully. Colognes and perfumes should not be overpowering.
- *Posture.* Sitting or standing, keep your shoulders back. Erect posture presents a professional image.
- *Fad or personal expression.* Piercings (other than ears) and tattoos do not convey a professional image and should not be visible to customers or other employees.

Communicating Effectively

Some people are natural communicators. But communication is a skill that can be improved with guidance and practice. The following are the most important points in being a successful communicator as a teller:

The first technique is to actively listen.

- Look at customers while they speak
- Want to listen better. It is in your best interest to hear all that customers have to say and to understand their needs.
- Listen to customers without interrupting. Be concerned about them and their banking needs so you will be in a position to recommend products
- Talk less. Listen more. You cannot speak and listen at the same time.
- Do not make any judgments or draw any conclusions while the customer is talking. While you are thinking about your conclusions it is very likely that you will miss part of what the customer is saying. You will have your chance to speak and to express your opinion later
- Remember that active listening is one of the best tools for building customer relationships and recognizing customer cues for additional banking needs

The second technique is to be conscious of what you say and how you say it.

- Pronounce the customer's name correctly. If you are not sure, ask
- Be conscious of the nonverbal messages you send, that is, messages you communicate through clothes, jewelry, grooming, facial expressions, eye contact, and the gestures of your body
- Avoid using bank language, or "jargon," that customers might not understand and that might make them feel inadequate. For example, would a customer understand if you said, "Your DDA is NSF. In order to avoid another OD fee, don't use any POS or ATM until we can process your EFT"?
- Take the time to explain procedures to customers as thoughtfully and as carefully as necessary, without treating them like children
- Avoid offensive expressions such as "You can't do that," "You have to," and "You're wrong." Substitute "I'm not sure if that's possible—let me check. I'm sure we'll be able to help you."
- On occasion, you will need to walk away or turn your back on a customer temporarily. When you do, excuse yourself first
- Be sincere, and be sure that sincerity is reflected in your voice
- Do not talk or complain about a customer's business or banking habits with anyone else, except as needed to conduct official bank business and even then, leave out the complaints. Stick to the facts

The third technique is to demonstrate professionalism and respect.

- Realize that many customers and bank employees speak English as a second language. These individuals should be made to feel confident as they develop their communication skills. Remember, you may need to speak a little more slowly, but you should not speak louder
- Treat all customers with the same respect no matter how they are dressed, how old they appear to be, what they look like, or what size their account is
- Respect any customer's preference for more personal privacy, anonymity, or social distance than you maintain with your more outgoing customers
- Be patient with customers who make mistakes, are slow in their thinking or motions, have forgotten to bring necessary documentation, or do not understand you or some procedures

EXERCISE 6-2   THE EFFECTIVE COMMUNICATOR

While you were reviewing the most important points for successful communication as a teller in the previous section, you were probably thinking about your own communication behaviors. How often do you practice the actions necessary to be a successful communicator? Following is a list of ten actions that the most effective tellers practice regularly. Probably no one does all these things all the time; how often do you do them?

For each statement, write the number that indicates how often you engage in that behavior. Be honest.

5 - almost always
4 - often
3 - sometimes
2 - infrequently
1 - hardly ever

____ 1. Before I speak, I visualize the exact response I want from the listener as a result of my words.
____ 2. When I speak, I adapt my words to the knowledge, language, mood, feelings, and motivation of my listener.
____ 3. I am careful to use concrete words and phrases that leave no doubt about my meaning.
____ 4. I pronounce my words accurately and distinctly.
____ 5. I know the impact of my nonverbal messages.
____ 6. Before I speak, I choose a time and a place consistent with the meaning I want to convey.
____ 7. I make eye contact when talking with others.
____ 8. I look and listen for feedback telling me whether I have been understood.
____ 9. When other people speak, I concentrate on their meaning.
____ 10. I avoid reacting to what people say until they have finished saying it.

Now add up the numbers for a total communication skills score

____ SCORE

If your score is	Your skill as a communicator
46–50	Outstanding.
40–45	Almost perfect.
30–39	You're on the right track.
29 or less	This module is for you!

Understanding the Customer's Needs

There are five basic steps you should follow to effectively respond to your customer's banking needs. These steps can be used when the customer specifically requests information on a product or complains about service.

1. **Greet the customer.** Smile, if appropriate. Working with a customer who has a complaint is probably not a good time to smile. Use the customer's name and show interest and enthusiasm. Example: "Good morning Mr. Webster. How may I help you today?"

2. **Actively listen to the customer's request.** Lean toward the customer, maintain eye contact, and listen for meaning to identify the customer's needs. Let the customer know you are listening by using phrases like "I see," "uh-huh," "ok," and so forth.

3. **Paraphrase and ask questions.** Restate the customer's concern, ask probing questions, and use the customer's name again. Example: "Mr. Webster, let me make sure I understand what happened. You made a deposit last Friday that has not shown up in your account balance yet. Is that correct? May I ask you where you made the deposit? Do you have the receipt with you? Did you use one of our tellers or an ATM machine?"

4. **Resolve the customer's concern.** Suggest an answer, offer a service, or make a referral. Example: "Mr. Webster, I can use the information you've given me to forward your question to our research department." In this situation, the teller offered to forward the customer's question to the appropriate bank department. If the customer has a question about a bank product or service, the teller would refer the customer to the appropriate specialist—such as a consumer loan officer or new accounts representative.

5. **Close the conversation on a positive note.** Thank the customer for using your bank, assure the customer you will follow up on the situation, use the customer's name. Example: "I'll follow up with them tomorrow afternoon and then I can call you to let you know what they've learned. At what number can you be reached between 3 and 4 o'clock?"

Note: Gaining product knowledge and understanding how banking regulations impact customers will help you to answer customer questions, address concerns, and refer customers to the appropriate bank personnel. You will learn about common bank products and key banking regulations later in this module.

Getting to Know Your Customers

Your first encounter with your customers will not give you enough information about them to know what they value most. It is up to you to interpret the clues they give you to identify which skills they find most important.

Your customers always give you clues. For example, pay attention to the small talk, or lack of small talk, as you process their transactions. If a customer does not share a lengthy response when you ask, "How are you today," he or she is probably not going to appreciate a lengthy greeting. Conversely, someone who responds with a lengthy answer to the same question will probably find your greeting an important part of the customer experience.

When you are learning about your customers, remember the following actions:

- Ask open-end questions to encourage them to share their interests and goals so you can learn about the type of accounts that would help them meet their needs
- Listen as they talk. It is easy to "tune out" in a normally hectic work environment. Remember, even short conversations can provide insight into what a customer finds important

Note: Check with your supervisor about the process for entering customer information into your bank's customer relationship management (CRM) system. Entering Information in the CRM system ensures that every user in every branch has access to the same information on the customer.

Adjusting Service Delivery to Meet Customer Expectations

Customers base their judgment of customer service delivery on how well their expectations are met. Customers who sense that you have recognized what is valuable to them, will feel more comfortable doing business with the bank.

You can adjust your customer service delivery to meet your customers' expectations. For instance, if your customer is always in a hurry, adjust your greeting to a quick, short, "Good morning Mrs. Evans." If Mrs. Evans likes to visit, then your greeting should be a little longer-"Good morning Mrs. Evans. How was your vacation?"

EXERCISE 6-3 ROLE-PLAYING EFFECTIVE COMMUNICATION

This exercise contains scenarios to "role-play" effective communications with customers. Write scripts for yourself, using the five steps of effective communication in understanding the customer's needs. After you complete the exercise, review your responses with your supervisor to ensure they follow your bank's specific guidelines.

Situation 1
Ms. Diego complains about an overdraft fee on her account. She has been a customer for seven years and this is the first time she overdrew her account.
Hint: Overdraft protection could save money.

Step 1: Greet the customer. You say:

Step 2: Actively listen to the customer's request. You do:

Step 3: Paraphrase and ask questions. You say:

Step 4: Resolve the customer's concern. You say:

Step 5: Close the conversation on a positive note. You say:

Situation 2
Dr. LoCoco, a long-time customer, wants to open an account for his new grandson.
Hint: The customer service representatives open all savings accounts.

Step 1: Greet the customer. You say:

Step 2: Actively listen to the customer's request. You do:

Step 3: Paraphrase and ask questions. You say:

Step 4: Resolve the customer's concern. You say:

Step 5: Close the conversation on a positive note. You say:

SECTION 3: DEALING WITH ALL KINDS OF CUSTOMERS

Your customer base will be composed of a variety of people—retired workers, young adults, educated professionals, people of different nationalities, and so on. All customers deserve to be treated with dignity and respect. You will look forward eagerly to serving 99.9 percent of your clients; the other 0.1 percent will present a challenge. These are the difficult customers who seem impossible to satisfy. With the right attitude, you can view a difficult client as a challenging opportunity. With the right skills, you can serve them effectively.

Sometimes a customer's difficulty will be totally explained by the situation, but occasionally you are going to serve an angry, cranky, nasty, or even disruptive customer. Difficult customers feel they have genuine complaints. They want to be heard and have their problems resolved. An empathetic, understanding teller goes a long way toward defusing an ugly situation.

The following four principles should rule your handling of difficult customers.

1. *Listen.* Listening, not speaking, is the best tool at your disposal. Listening, and perhaps a little questioning, helps you learn what is wrong in a situation and what the customer is feeling. Listening also helps you to calm an angry customer because it allows him or her to express feelings. Even if what the customer is saying is wrong, you should listen as long as you can without speaking. You cannot begin to reason with an angry customer until he or she has calmed down. Allowing the customer a few minutes to express his or her feelings is the first step to helping him or her calm down.

2. *Stay calm.* Never allow yourself to look angry or upset, and do not argue with the customer. Getting angry yourself and arguing only escalates a difficult situation. Maintain a calm appearance even if you do not feel calm inside. Do not let the customer rile you or make you rush. Be firm, polite, and tactful. Distance yourself personally from critical or abusive customers, even while you listen intently to what they say.

3. *Solve what you can.* Do not attempt to resolve complaints unless you have the authority to make the necessary adjustments. If you need help resolving the customer's situation, introduce the customer to a supervisor or to an appropriate bank employee. A good strategy here is reflected by such a statement as "We need to find a bank officer who can give this matter the attention it deserves; please have a seat while I get us some help."

4. *Follow bank policy.* When you do have the experience and authority to handle the problem yourself, follow the bank's policies and procedures to the letter. Describe the applicable bank policy carefully (without using the words "bank policy") and give the reasons behind it. Explain that the procedures you are following are in place to protect the customer's money.

EXERCISE 6-4 THE DIFFICULT CUSTOMER

Imagine that you are in your teller station serving a customer you do not recognize. It is a busy day at the bank, with a longer-than-average waiting line. How would you respond in each of the following situations? What would you say? What would you do?

1. An impatient customer waiting in line complains loudly in your direction about not being served sooner. He says angrily, "What's it take to get served around here? Does anyone know what they're doing?"

2. A customer balks at your having to get approval to cash her check. She complains, "What do you mean, you'll have to get that check approved? My family has been doing business with this bank for forty years!"

3. An irate customer throws his monthly checking account statement down on the counter and says, "This is the second time this year you've screwed up my records with your stupid computer. You make good money off my account, and I want satisfaction now!"

SECTION 4: PRODUCT KNOWLEDGE SKILLS

Banking is a service industry that offers products to satisfy the needs of consumer and business customers. Most banks offer similar products with slight variations in individual features. As a teller, you should focus on learning the features of your bank's products and how those features can benefit your customers. This will help you to recognize customer cues that indicate a need for an additional product or service.

Important: Remember, the main characteristic that differentiates your bank from the competitors is the quality of service your customers receive.

Cross-selling bank products and services has become a job skill required for every position in the bank. As a teller, your focus will be on listening for cues from customers regarding needs and referring them to the appropriate person in the branch for additional products and services to meet those needs. The more you know about a product or service, the easier it will be to determine which product or service would meet the needs of a customer and to explain the product or refer the customer to the appropriate person or area. It is more important to mention the benefits of a product/service, than to list the features of the product/service.

In this section, you will learn about common bank products and services and how to recognize opportunities for making referrals.

Checking Accounts

Personal Checking Accounts

Most customers choose to have at least one checking account. The account may be individual or joint with another party. Checking accounts provide a safe, secure method for paying third parties. Each month the bank issues a statement to aid the customer's record keeping. Customers may make deposits or withdrawals at any time. If a check is lost, the customer has the right to stop payment on those funds for a fee. Most checking accounts may be accessed via an automated teller machine, online banking, and mobile banking. Personal checking accounts have the option to pay interest on available funds. Monthly account maintenance fees may be assessed. The Federal Deposit Insurance Corporation (FDIC) insures funds based on account ownership.

Business Checking Accounts

This type of account has many of the same features as a personal checking account. The account enables a business to make third-party payments. Many banks offer additional services specific to the needs of businesses. Funds may be insured based on the type of ownership for the business account.

Savings Accounts

Personal Savings Accounts

Savings accounts earn interest, which is paid at regular intervals. The most common types of savings accounts are statement savings accounts and money market savings accounts. Statement savings customers receive a periodic statement listing all transactions. The FDIC insures the funds in savings accounts, which provides peace of mind to bank customers.

Business Savings Accounts

These accounts are savings accounts that have been designed with the small business customer in mind. Periodic statements provide a recap of banking activity. Funds may be insured based on the type of ownership for the business account.

ATM and Debit Cards

Banks issue ATM and debit cards so that customers have more convenient opportunities to deposit and withdraw cash.

An ATM card is a plastic card, issued by a bank, that can be used only to obtain cash at any ATM or to make deposits at the issuing bank's proprietary ATMs.

A debit card (sometimes called a check card) can perform all the functions of an ATM card, and more. It is generally either a Visa or MasterCard, branded with the bank's personalized card name. A debit card looks like a credit card and is accepted as payment for purchases wherever that brand is accepted. The difference between a debit card and a credit card is that, for a debit card, the amount of the purchase is deducted directly from the customer's checking account rather than billed to the customer on a monthly basis as happens with credit cards. The effect of using a debit card is the same as if the customer wrote a check, but the transaction is much simpler.

Debit cards can be used either by entering a PIN (Personal Identification Number) on a key touch pad or by signing a sales slip, similar to authorizing a credit card transaction. For the consumer, the only difference between the two transactions is supplying a PIN or a signature, but both types of transactions debit the customer's account, often immediately.

Prepaid Debit Cards

Most banks issue prepaid cards, and this device is rapidly becoming a major payment tool. A prepaid card is a plastic debit card that looks like a credit card, but instead of debiting the customer's bank account, the funds are accessed through an implanted computer chip in the card. After the value on a prepaid card has been spent, some cards can be "reloaded" with additional monetary value and used again. For example, the Visa BUXX® card marketed to teens is a prepaid, reloadable Visa card that parents can use to teach teens how to create a budget, manage money, and shop wisely. Parents and other family members can fund the card, and they can also monitor their teen's spending. Parents can set the spending limits by the prepaid amount loaded on the card.

Payroll Cards

Banks are always looking for ways to meet the needs of their customers. For example, some customers are unable to open checking accounts or find that checking accounts are too expensive and, therefore, take their paychecks to check-cashing stores. One increasingly popular product, payroll cards, meets the needs of people from low to high income. A payroll card is a prepaid, reloadable plastic card that holds an employee's weekly pay. It can be used like any other debit card to pay for groceries, gas, or services at a store or to obtain cash at an ATM. Such cards are particularly useful for over-the-road truckers, for example, who would have problems accessing their funds while on the road. These are also good for minors working a part time job and are too young to open an account at a bank, or anyone who finds it difficult to open an account or cash a check. Employers may benefit from better record keeping and avoiding the expense of issuing paper checks. Although tellers seldom issue payroll cards, holders of these cards may come to you for a cash advance. Tellers need to know that users of payroll cards are protected against fraud and unauthorized access under the Electronic Funds Transfer Act Regulation E.

Certificates of Deposit

Offered to both consumers and business customers, certificates of deposit (CDs)—also called time deposits (TDs)—consist of funds deposited into an account for a specified period during which the customer cannot withdraw without penalty and on which the bank agrees to pay a guaranteed rate of interest for that period. These accounts typically earn a higher rate of interest than a savings account. As with savings accounts, CDs are FDIC insured.

Safe Deposit Boxes

Safe deposit boxes are strong metal containers for valuables such as jewelry or documents, usually kept in a bank vault. Safe deposit boxes have the following features:

- A popular, inexpensive service for customers
- Provide protection against fire and water damage to contents
- Secure due to strict security procedures followed to gain access to a box
  - Some banks require two keys to open a box—one bank key and one customer key
  - Other banks use equipment that scans your hand or eyes to verify identity
- Typically located in an individual locked compartment in the bank vault (other banks offer a self-service type of box that requires only one key and permits customers to enter and exit without signing a log)
- Rented by individuals or by businesses
- Not covered by FDIC insurance because the contents of the boxes are not known to the bank

Loans / Lines of Credit

Banks offer a variety of loan products to meet customer needs. There are two general types of loan products: installment loans and lines of credit.

Installment Loans

Installment loans are repaid with a fixed number of equal payments. For example, 60 monthly payments of $150.00 each. Three common types of installment loans are

- Auto loan—Funds are used purchase a new or used vehicle
- Mortgage loan—Funds are used to purchase or refinance property or real estate
- Home equity loan—Funds can be used for a variety of worthwhile purposes such as paying off higher interest rate credit cards, paying school tuition, or paying for an expensive vacation

Lines of Credit

Lines of credit function like a credit card. The customer is approved for a maximum amount of credit and can borrow against that amount as needed. The monthly payment amount will vary depending on the amount borrowed on the line of credit.

A home equity line of credit is one very popular example. Like a home equity loan, a home equity line of credit can be used for a variety of purposes. It is a very flexible type of loan product, as the customer can borrow whatever amount is needed at any given time (up to the credit limit).

Other Products and Services

Business Loans and Cash Management Services

Banks can offer businesses many types of products and services to help the owners manage cash flow and fund business expenses. Typically, there are business specialists within the bank who work with the business owners to identify products and services to meet the businesses' financial needs.

Trust Services

Some banks offer trust services, which focus on the management of financial assets (estate planning).

Insurance Products

Banks may work through affiliates to offer insurance products such as home insurance and auto insurance.

College Savings Accounts

A savings account set up with the specific purpose of saving money for college expenses. Certain types of college savings accounts may have income tax advantages, depending on the customer's situation.

Common Bank Products and Services

Take the time to learn and know the features and benefits of the range of products and services offered by your bank. Research shows that the more services a customer uses at your bank, the more loyal the customer is and the less likely that customer is to change to a competitor institution.

Exhibit 6-2 lists the most common bank products and services. Take note of which services are offered by your bank.

Exhibit 6-2 Common Bank Products and Services

PRODUCTS

Deposit

- Checking accounts (commercial and personal)
- Savings accounts
- Money market accounts
- Certificates of deposit (CDs)
- Retirement savings accounts (IRAs)
- Education savings accounts
- Health savings

Loans

- Personal loans
- Commercial loans
- Small Business Administration (SBA) loans
- Small business loans
- Automobile loans
- Mortgages and home equity loans
- Credit cards
- Lines of credit

Payroll cards

Gift cards/checks

Prepaid cards

Insurance (home, health, life, credit life, automobile)

Investment

- Annuities
- Savings bonds

SERVICES

Direct deposit

Automated teller machines (ATMs)

Debit card

Money orders

Certified checks

Cashier's checks

Traveler's checks

Overdraft protection

Safe deposit boxes

Night depository services

Lock box services

Online banking and bill payment

Wire transfer

Financial planning

Foreign currency exchange

Trust and estate planning

Automated Clearing House (ACH) services

Cash management

Signature guarantees

Notary services

Fraud and identity theft services

Online banking

Telephone banking

Mobile banking

Mobile deposit

EXERCISE 6-5   ONE STEP AHEAD OF THE COMPETITION

1. Working with your teller trainer or lead teller, list up to ten of the most common services offered by your bank.

2. As a result of competition with other types of financial institutions, what two new services has your bank started offering in recent years?

3. What new services do you think your bank should develop to remain competitive?

Making Referrals

As you become more experienced in your job and more comfortable processing customer transactions, your bank may expect you to begin referring customers to other areas of the bank for products and services offered by your bank. Making referrals involves listening to cues from customers about their needs and then referring them to the appropriate person. As a "frontline" person who sees more customers than anyone else in the bank, you are in a unique position to know what your customers need and refer them to other bank employees who can help them, perhaps by opening additional accounts or providing necessary services. This process deepens the customer's relationship with the bank and creates a happier, more satisfied and loyal customer.

Many banks reward tellers for referrals—by recognition, monetary rewards, promotions, or all three. To make successful referrals, you need to know what products or services your bank offers and understand the clues a customer might present.

See the table on the following page for some ideas.

Situation	Referral
Mrs. Garcia comments that her CD is almost up for renewal and she is not happy with the current interest rates.	Ask Mrs. Garcia if she would like to speak to someone in your investment area about other investment options. Be sure to say that such products are not FDIC-insured. ***Do not make recommendations!*** (Even if you know that someone had particular luck with a stock purchase or mutual fund investment, you are not a licensed investment advisor and you must not make recommendations.)
Ms. Patel mentions that she will be tackling some home improvement projects soon, including a new kitchen.	Ask Ms. Patel if she would like to hear about loan options and refer her to a loan officer.
Mr. Dietz comments that his father just passed away and he is coming into a large inheritance.	Refer Mr. Dietz to your Trust department.
Aisha and her fiancé are getting married soon and are thinking about buying a house.	Refer Aisha to a mortgage loan officer.
Marco notes that his auto insurance rates are going up—again.	Refer Marco to your insurance affiliate. (Be careful here—there are required disclosures for insurance referrals—check with your manager to see how your bank handles this.)
Sasha complains that her car broke down for the third time this month!	Refer Sasha to a loan officer for a new car loan.
Michelle tells you that in a year her son will be going to college.	Refer Michelle to a loan officer to discuss loan options.
Mr. Lopez states that his daughter just had a baby and he is a proud grandpa.	Ask Mr. Lopez if he would be interested in opening an account, such as a college savings account, for the baby.
Roland's business is growing faster than he ever imagined. He is not sure how to proceed, but he knows he needs credit and possibly cash management services.	Refer Roland to your business specialist.

Situation	Referral
Olga is hiring a caretaker for her elderly mother, but she is worried about the valuables in the house with strangers coming in and out all the time.	Refer Olga for a safe deposit box.

EXERCISE 6-6   OTHER BANK PRODUCTS

Fill in the chart with information about three products your bank offers that you believe will be popular with customers. See exhibit 6-2 for ideas.

Generic product name	Your bank's product name	Product features	Product benefits
Example ATM Card	"Anytime 24"	Accesses accounts, permits transactions, 24 hours a day	Safety convenience

EXERCISE 6-7 WHICH BANK PRODUCT BEST SUITS MY CUSTOMER?

Which of these products will satisfy these customers' needs?

    a. installment loan
    b. personal checking account
    c. business savings account
    d. personal savings account
    e. business checking account
    f. safe deposit box

____ 1. Each week, this customer cashes her paycheck at your bank.

____ 2. A customer complains that his car is always breaking down.

____ 3. A customer mentions that she just started a small business and needs a way to keep the money she receives from customers separate from her personal checking account.

____ 4. A customer tells you she carries around savings bonds and stock certificates in her purse.

____ 5. A customer expresses her joy at having won $5,000 in the lottery.

____ 6. You notice the balance is always unusually high in the Harry's Hamburgers, Inc., checking account. No interest is earned on this checking account.

JOB AID 6-1   SALES AND SERVICE GUIDE

Using exhibit 6-2 as a guide, collect all your bank's current brochures on its products and services. Go through each brochure and highlight the features that will appeal to your customers. Put the brochures in a three-ring binder (or create a digital folder and download the brochures) with tabs for the following major headings:

- Checking and related services
- Savings and investment services
- Loan services
- Protection of assets
- Retirement planning

For each product or service, consider the information that will enable you to 1) determine the types of customers who would benefit from the product or service and 2) discuss the product or service with your customers. For example, consider the following information:

- Product/service description (what does it do for the customer?)
- Target customers (who would most benefit from the product or service?)
- Key features (characteristics such as minimum deposit required, etc.)
- Key benefits (value of the features in terms of saving time, saving/earning money, providing convenience, etc.)

To add supplemental information, make as many copies as you need of the sample "product guide" form on the following page.

TIP: Review the completed binder with your manager. Update the brochures as needed.

PRODUCT GUIDE

Product: _____

Description: _____

Target customer (demographic description, deposit level): _____

_____

_____

Minimum deposit to open: _____

Minimum balance to avoid monthly service charge: _____

Minimum balance to earn interest: _____

Interest rate base: _____

When does rate change? _____

Interest accrual method: _____

When is interest paid? _____

Other fees: _____

Other features: _____

JOB AID 6-2   INCLUSIVE REFERENCE LIST

In order to make a referral, you need to know who your internal bank partners are to whom you would refer the customer for certain products or services.

Create an *Inclusive Reference List* as your personal reference list for referrals. Many new tellers find this list to be another valuable tool as they get to know the other people in their branch that are experts in certain products and services.

Create a reference tool that will help you be effective in performing your job. Create lists, a card file, or a manual including all of the following:

- *Phone numbers* called most often, including bank departments to which you may refer a customer regarding a particular service
- *Security information*, including robbery data and emergency phone numbers, such as those for the police and fire department
- *Identification requirements*
- *Check-cashing guidelines*, including teller limits for negotiating checks
- *A pictorial of the initials or signatures of bank officers who are authorized to approve checks.* Some banks create a list of the names of the bank's officers and have the officers initial and write their signature next to their name. Other banks provide a list of bank officers' initials in which each initial is followed by a code that is changed regularly as a security precaution. Copies of this sheet of paper are provided to the tellers to be kept in a secure location
- *A list of businesses that do not bank with you but whose checks you cash*
- *Any other information you use regularly*

Keep the completed list in the Sales and Service Guide you created earlier.

SECTION 5: HELPING YOUR CUSTOMERS UNDERSTAND THE RULES

When tellers learn about compliance, they are usually trained on the Bank Secrecy Act (BSA) and how to complete a Currency Transaction Report (CTR). Compliance is much more than that—it really is just good customer service! Although you do not need to know all the ins and outs of every banking law and regulation, you do need to know some key points in order to be able to answer customers' questions and meet your customers' needs.

This section covers the regulations that directly affect your customers' access to their funds or the transactions they can request using their funds. It is important to be able to explain to customers the intent of these regulations so they will understand why they are in place.

Regulation CC

This regulation mandates that banks make funds from deposited items available to customers within a specific time. Be sure that you can explain to a customer the difference between check funds being "available" and a check being "good." Being "good" means that the check will not bounce due to insufficient funds in the check writer's account. Many customers have been financially harmed when funds from fraudulent cashier's checks and other checks they deposited were made available to them shortly after deposit, but the checks were later returned as fraudulent.

What Does This Mean for You?

Be sure you can explain to your customers that if the check was received from a person they do not know well, they must be cautious because they are ultimately liable and a fraudulent check will be charged back against their account.

Customers who indicate that they are being directed to deposit the check, withdraw funds when they become available, and wire them to another account should be directed to speak to management. It is highly likely the transaction is fraudulent.

Regulation D

Under Regulation D, customers are limited to six third-party withdrawals (electronic funds transfers, direct debits, telephone transfers, or checks) per month or statement cycle for money market or savings accounts. If the customer exceeds these limits, your bank may close the savings account, prevent future third-party withdrawals, or convert the account to a transaction account (demand deposit) such as a checking account.

What Does This Mean for You?

Your bank probably has a policy regarding excess transfers from savings accounts and either imposes a fee on customers who exceed the limits or prevents the excess transfers by returning the item. This causes a great inconvenience to your customers, who may not understand or like all the rules and regulations that pertain to their accounts.

What Can You Do?

You can suggest that the customer use a withdrawal ticket rather than a check to withdraw funds from his own money market account, when the customer is at your teller window. In-person withdrawals are unlimited and will not count against your customer's limited withdrawals for the month or statement cycle. You can save your customer time, cost, inconvenience, and aggravation by understanding your bank's policy as it pertains to this regulation.

Regulation E

Regulation E establishes the rights, liabilities, and responsibilities of parties in electronic funds transfers (which are transactions involving debit cards, ATM cards, online banking, mobile banking and EFT services) and protects consumers (not business customers) when they use such systems.

What Does This Mean for You?

If a customer has lost his/her ATM card, has a missing direct deposit, or does not recognize some transactions on his/her statement, you need to take action immediately! Check with your supervisor to see what your bank's policy is regarding Regulation E notification. Some banks have forms that the customer must complete; others will accept verbal notification.

Remember—a customer's mention of a problem is considered "notifying" the bank of the problem, so you must be sure the customer's concerns are handled appropriately.

Regulation DD

Regulation DD implements the Truth in Savings Act and requires depository institutions to provide disclosures to enable consumers to make meaningful comparisons of deposit accounts.

What Does This Mean for You?

When disclosing interest rates to customers, you must tell them the annual percentage rate and the annual percentage yield.

- You must say "annual percentage rate" and "annual percentage yield"—rather than APR and APY
- No other rates may be stated

If the customer asks for something in writing, most banks give the customer a copy of the current rate sheet, which contains all the appropriate disclosures. Ask your supervisor where to obtain consumer rate sheets and to explain your bank's policy regarding customer inquiries.

Regulation B

Regulation B is a lending regulation that implements the Equal Credit Opportunity Act. The purpose of this regulation, in part, is to promote the availability of credit (loans and lines of credit) to all creditworthy applicants without regard to race, color, religion, national origin, sex, marital status, or age (provided the applicant has the capacity to contract). The regulation prohibits creditor practices that discriminate on the basis of any of these factors.

What Does This Mean for You?

Very often, tellers are approached by individuals wanting information about credit products offered by the bank. It is important to remember to ***treat all potential applicants equally by encouraging them to apply***.

Even if you know the customer's account is always overdrawn or that the customer is unemployed, you must encourage the customer to apply if the customer asks for an application. Do not discourage the applicant or indicate in any way that the person will not be approved. (If the customer is denied credit, an appropriate notice will be sent by your loan department.)

The only exception to this rule is if the customer is under the legal age or if the customer is asking for a loan product your bank does not offer. For example, if the customer needs a loan to purchase an airplane and your bank does not make airplane loans, you may tell the customer that is not a loan you offer. However, you might encourage the customer to apply for another type of loan such as a home equity loan or an unsecured loan that would allow the customer to use the proceeds to purchase the airplane. Ask your supervisor how your bank expects tellers to respond to loan requests.

Community Reinvestment Act

The Community Reinvestment Act (CRA) was enacted by Congress to encourage banks subject to this law to help meet the credit needs of the local communities in which the institution is chartered, including low- and moderate-income neighborhoods.

The purpose of the CRA is to provide credit—including home ownership opportunities—to underserved populations and commercial loans to small businesses.

As part of CRA, a bank is required to maintain a Public File containing the following items:

- Written comments received from the public
- Copy of the public lesson of the bank's most recent CRA performance evaluation
- List of the bank's branches, with street addresses
- List of branches opened or closed by the bank during the current year and each of the prior two calendar years
- List of services (including hours of operation, available loan and deposit products, and transaction fees) generally offered at the bank's branches

What Do You Need to Know?

You should know who your bank's CRA officer is (the name and contact information) and where the Public File for your bank is located. Occasionally individuals, businesses, or consumer groups may ask for a copy of your Public File. Ask your supervisor what your bank's policy is regarding such requests.

Regulation P

Regulation P governs how your bank handles the privacy of consumer financial information. It governs how financial institutions use nonpublic personal information about consumers. Although this regulation does not cover commercial (business) customers, ask your supervisor about your bank's policy and be prepared to explain it to your customers if you are asked.

What Does This Mean for You?

You need to be cognizant of your customer's privacy at all times. It is important to remember not to inadvertently divulge protected information about your customer to other customers and even to other employees. For example, do not yell to another teller "Hey Joe…can I buy $10,000 in large bills from you so I can cash Mr. Jones' disability check?" The following actions will help protect customer privacy:

- Be sure to dispose of any confidential customer information appropriately. Do not place it in the trash!
- Clean up around your work area and clear your screen before helping a new customer
- Never discuss your prior customer's transactions with the next customer in line

Federal Deposit Insurance Corporation

When transacting business, customers may ask you if your bank's deposits are insured. They are referring to the U.S. government-backed insurance company known as the Federal Deposit Insurance Corporation (FDIC).

The FDIC is an independent agency of the U.S. government. It was established by Congress in 1933 to insure bank deposits and thereby help maintain sound conditions in our banking system and protect the nation's money supply in case of bank failure. In 1989, the FDIC was given the added responsibility of insuring deposits in savings associations. Each bank pays for the cost of the insurance through semiannual assessments based on the volume of deposits. All types of deposits received by the bank in its usual course of business are insured.

What Does This Mean for You?

The basic insured amount for a depositor is $250,000. Under certain conditions, a customer may qualify for more than the established coverage at one insured bank. Explanations of FDIC insurance coverage can be long and complicated. For this reason, many banks ask tellers to refer questions about it to a personal banker who can sit down and spend a little more time with a customer to answer questions specifically related to the customer's account status.

Some depositors are concerned about the FDIC coverage limit and may wish to move some of their deposits to other financial institutions to receive more coverage. Refer questions about FDIC coverage to your manager for advice. In addition, many banks provide annual training on FDIC coverage. Be sure to participate in these training programs when they are made available to you.

Another resource available to both consumers and bankers is the FDIC's Electronic Deposit Insurance Estimator (EDIE) accessed through the FDIC website: https://www5.fdic.gov/edie/

The estimator can be used to calculate FDIC coverage based on specific deposit scenarios.

Your Future

In the financial world, flexibility in the organization and its staff is the key to success. Keep your skills updated.

Twenty years ago, a teller simply paid out cash and accepted deposits; now many tellers are responsible for soliciting accounts and explaining services. Customers expect you to know the answers to their questions. Staying abreast of industry news and services through training will lead you down the road to success.

MODULE 6 REVIEW QUIZ

1. What are the five elements of a professional appearance?

2. What is your best tool for handling difficult customers?

3. What are the four principles to follow when handling difficult customers?

4. What are three general techniques that tellers can use to foster effective communication with customers?

5. What are at least three things you can do to make you customers feel valued?

6. What are the three components of quality service?

7. What action might customers take if tellers do not keep them informed of new products and services?

8. How many times should you try to use a customer's name during a transaction?

9. What are the five steps you should follow to effectively respond to a customer's banking needs?

10. What product would you recommend to a customer who carries excessive valuables in a briefcase?

11. What type of loan do customers generally request for purchasing a car?

12. What product would you recommend to a customer who purchases money orders to pay bills?

13. Are the contents of a safe deposit box insured by the FDIC?

14. Why was the Truth in Savings Act (Reg DD) enacted?

ANSWERS TO EXERCISES

Exercise 6-4: The Difficult Customer

1. Acknowledge the customer. Assure the customer that you will call a manager to assist. Call a manager.
2. Do not take this as a personal attack. Do not cut off the customer if she wants to keep talking. Explain that the reason for getting the check approved is to protect the customer.
3. This is probably not a problem a teller can solve. Listen to the customer, but do not lead him on as though you could solve the problem. Call for a supervisor or customer service representative, and assure the customer you are referring him to someone who can help him more effectively.

Exercise 6-7: Which Bank Product Best Suits My Customer?

1. b
2. a
3. e
4. f
5. d
6. c

Appendix A: Glossary

Acceptability—In addition to being negotiable, a check must meet acceptability requirements. For example, checks may not be postdated (dated in the future) or stale-dated (date is more than six months old).

Account—An arrangement with a bank to hold money and keep records of transactions.

Affiliate—An affiliate is an organization (such as an insurance company) which is officially connected with another, larger organization (such as a bank).

Altered currency—Currency that has been changed or tampered with to obtain more for the currency than its face value.

Annual percentage yield (APY)—A percentage rate reflecting the total amount of interest to be earned on an interest-bearing deposit account, based on the interest rate and the frequency of compounding.

ATM card—A card that allows a customer to withdraw or deposit funds, check balances, or perform other services at an ATM machine. Unlike debit cards, an ATM card cannot be used to pay for purchases.

Bait money—Paper currency, usually kept separate from other currency in the cash drawer, that is to be included with the currency given out during a robbery. Serial numbers of the bills are recorded for use in suspect identification and conviction.

Balance—Amount of funds in an account.

Bankcard—A credit card issued by a bank, allowing the client to use the ATM and make credit purchases with a preapproved available line of credit. Visa and MasterCard are the most common bankcards.

Bank security officer—Employee of a bank who is trained to oversee the bank security program and to protect employees, customers, and property

Business day—Monday through Friday, except Federal banking holidays.

Cash-in—Cash received.

Cash-out—Cash distributed.

Check—An instrument that contains an unconditional order from the account owner that directs a bank to pay a specific amount of money to a payee. Generally, the money is drawn from a checking account.

Check clearing—The movement of a check from the depository institution at which it was deposited back to the institution on which it was written; the movement of funds in the opposite direction and the corresponding credit and debit to the involved accounts.

Counterfeit—Made in exact imitation of something valuable or important to be passed off as genuine with the intention to deceive or defraud.

Credit—To add an amount of money to an account. Also, a contractual agreement in which a borrower receives funds now (or has access to funds as needed) and agrees to repay the lender at some date in the future, generally with interest.

Cross-selling—Encouraging an existing customer to make use of additional bank products or services.

Customer expectations—The services customers expect to find in a bank and, especially, how they anticipate being treated.

Debit—A charge against a bank deposit account.

Debit card—Plastic card used as a credit card to pay for purchases, and ATMs. Funds used to cover the purchases are withdrawn automatically from the customer's checking or savings account. Visa and MasterCard supply this service to banks. Transactions are reported on a customer's monthly statement.

Demand deposit—Funds that are available to the customer at any time and that require no advance notice of withdrawal. Checking accounts are the most common form of demand deposits.

Deposit—To leave money or items with a bank for credit to a bank account.

Deposit slip—A form on which a customer lists cash and checks to be deposited.

Depositary bank—The bank in which a check is first deposited. The bank also may be the drawee if the check is drawn on, payable at, or payable through the bank.

Difficult customer—A customer who presents problems that cannot be solved; expresses excessive or overly aggressive anger through disruptive or threatening behavior.

Drawee—Generally, the bank of the person writing the check. The drawee is also referred to as the check writer's bank.

Drawn on—In banking terms, "drawn on" means that a check is written on an account at a bank and funds from that account are used to pay the check.

Dual control—A situation in which two persons work together to verify each other's work. Method of maintaining security whereby two individuals must be present during transactions involving risk. Dual control for locked or secured areas is accomplished through the proper segregation of key and combination assignments for entry into secured areas.

Dye pack—A dye pack is a radio-controlled incendiary device used by banks to foil a robbery by causing stolen cash to be permanently marked with dye shortly after a robbery. In most cases, a dye pack is placed in a hollowed-out space within a stack of banknotes, usually $10 or $20 bills.

Endorsement—Signature(s) or words written or stamped on the back of a check that allow the payee to deposit or cash the check.

Extortion—The crime of obtaining money, property, or a promise by threat or intimidation.

Federal Deposit Insurance Corporation (FDIC) —Federal agency organized in 1933 to guarantee funds on deposit in member banks. The FDIC insures deposits at banks through the Bank Insurance Fund (BIF) and insures deposits at savings associations through the Savings Association Insurance Fund (SAIF).

Federal Reserve System (the Fed) —Central banking system that regulates the supply of money. It includes 12 regional "bankers' banks," their branches, and all national and state banks that choose to be members.

Finance charge—The cost of credit. Total of all costs a customer must pay for obtaining credit.

Forgery—The alteration of a document or instrument with fraudulent intent.

Fraud—An attempt to obtain funds by other than appropriate and legal means.

Grace period—Stipulated time, following the date on which payment is due, during which no late fee is charged.

Guaranteed funds—Funds that are immediately available with no possibility of loss. For example, funds withdrawn from the customer's available account balance would be guaranteed funds.

Hold—A hold means that the bank will not release a certain amount of the funds to the customer for a specific period of time.

Identification—It is imperative that tellers confirm the identity of anyone to whom they are giving out cash or information. A withdrawal completed or check cashed without adequate identification places the teller and the bank at great risk. You must

- Verify the identity of the person requesting the withdrawal, asking to cash a check, or asking for cash back from a deposit
- Be sure that the customer is legally entitled to withdraw funds from the account
- Ascertain that there are sufficient funds in the account

Interest—The amount paid by a borrower to a lender in exchange for the use of the lender's money over a certain period; can also be the amount paid to a depositor on a deposit or savings account.

Investment—The exchange of money for a promise to repay at a later date, or for an ownership share in a business venture.

Kidnapping—Criminal offense in which a person is seized and held involuntarily.

Kiting—Attempt to draw against nonexistent funds through a scheme involving several checking accounts with different institutions.

Lending—Giving out money temporarily on the condition that the full amount plus interest be repaid within a specified time period.

Loan—A business contract by which a borrower and a lender enter into an agreement.

Maker—This is the person who wrote and signed the check, authorizing the bank to transfer funds to the payee. The maker may be one or more individuals acting on their own behalf or authorized to act on behalf of a business, organization, or governmental agency. The maker is also referred to as the check writer or drawer.

Money—Coins and currency declared by a government to be the accepted medium of exchange.

Money order—A money order is a check drawn by a bank on itself or another bank. Money orders are also sold by the United States Postal Service, grocery stores, convenience stores, and companies such as Western Union® and MoneyGram®. They are used most often by customers who either do not have checking accounts or must have guaranteed funds (for example, to make a rent payment). A money order is most often negotiable, acceptable, and guaranteed by the bank to be good up to the amount specified on the money order.

Negotiable—Transferable by endorsement. A negotiable item can be exchanged for cash by meeting federal regulations and individual bank standards.

Negotiable instrument—A legal written document promising to pay another person or entity a certain amount of money. The most common form of negotiable instrument is a check.

Negotiable item—Items like cashier's checks, gift cards, and money orders. A negotiable item can be exchanged for cash by meeting federal regulations and individual bank standards.

Next-day availability—Funds deposited must be made available on the next business day following the day of deposit.

Office of the Comptroller of the Currency—Official of the United States government, appointed by the president and confirmed by the Senate, responsible for chartering, examining, supervising, and liquidating national banks.

Official check—An official check, also called a cashier's check, bank check, or treasurer's check, is a check drawn by a bank on itself. There is no maximum issue amount for a cashier's check. However, tellers often have individual limits on the dollar amount they can issue without approval. Cashier's checks are used by customers who require guaranteed funds, such as for home closing costs or purchasing a car. Cashier's checks are also given to customers who are closing a bank account and want to deposit the funds at another financial institution.

On-us check—A check deposited at the bank on which it is drawn.

Open-end questions—Questions that encourage a longer response and typically cannot be answered with a simple "yes" or "no." For example: "Tell me about…" and "What do you like best about…"

Payee—The recipient of the funds. The payee can be one or more individuals, a business, organization, government agency, cash, or bearer.

Payroll card—A prepaid, reloadable plastic card that holds the employees' weekly payroll. It can be used like any other debit card to pay for groceries, gas, services at a store, or to obtain cash at an ATM.

Product benefit—An advantage that a product feature creates for a customer.

Product feature—A characteristic or an element of a product.

Professionalism—Highest standards of behavior and performance.

Quality service—An excellent level of service provided to customers.

Referral—Directing a potential customer from one area of the bank, such as the teller window, to another area, such as consumer lending, to help the customer obtain information about or purchase another product or service.

Returned check—A check that is not paid by the bank on which it is written. A check is not paid if there are not enough funds in the account (referred to as "NSF" or not sufficient funds). A check will also be returned if the account is closed.

Satisfied customer—A result of meeting customer expectations and a cause of increased business for the bank.

- Customer expectations + meet expectations = satisfied customer
- Customer expectations + exceed expectations = highly satisfied customer

Substitute check—A paper reproduction of the original check drawn from an electronic file that contains an image of the front and back. It bears the full MICR line as allowed by industry standards for such checks, conforms in paper stock and dimensions to the standards, and can be processed through automated check systems.

Traveler's check—In the past, traveler's checks were frequently used by individuals traveling on vacation to foreign countries to purchase goods and services, and to exchange for local currency. However, with the increasing use of credit and debit cards, along with the availability of ATMs worldwide, traveler's checks are no longer common.

Uncollected funds—The portion of the account balance that includes check amounts that have not yet cleared.

Appendix B: Routing Transit Number: Federal Reserve Districts and Branch Cities

The routing transit numbers on the bottom and upper right corner of the check should match the Federal Reserve District of the drawee bank location: The first two numbers in the routing transit number at the bottom of the check will be the Federal Reserve district number where the drawee bank is located. For example, **a check drawn against a bank located in the western part of the United States will have a routing transit number that begins with the number 12.** The chairman of the Federal Reserve Board plays an immensely important role in the U.S. economy. Other regulatory agencies are listed in appendix D.

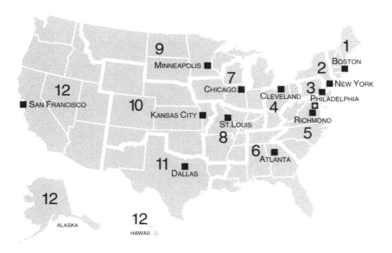

APPENDIX C: FEDERAL RESERVE SYSTEM

The Federal Reserve System of the United States is the central bank; it controls all currency and demand deposit exchanges between banks in the United States. The system also regulates the supply of money and the issuance of paper money.

The Federal Reserve System consists of the board of governors, 12 Federal Reserve banks, member commercial banks, and the Federal Open Market Committee.

Twelve banking districts, each with its own Federal Reserve bank, make up the Federal Reserve System (see below). **Each of the 12 districts is assigned a number and corresponding letter (1 is A, 2 is B, and so forth). The letters appear on U.S. currency.**

APPENDIX D: REGULATORY AGENCIES

In addition to the Federal Reserve Board, several other regulators and regulatory agencies monitor banks and other financial institutions.

Office of the Comptroller of the Currency (OCC)—An independent bureau within the U.S. Treasury Department that is responsible for chartering, examining, and supervising all national banks and federal savings associations.

Federal Deposit Insurance Corporation (FDIC)—Federal agency organized in 1933 that insures depositor's accounts at most commercial banks and thrift institutions. The FDIC is the primary regulator of insured state-chartered commercial banks that are not members of the Federal Reserve System and state-chartered savings associations.

State Regulatory Agencies—State agencies that supervise state-chartered banks. They are responsible for chartering and examining banks, constructing and enforcing bank regulations, and ruling on branch and merger applications.

Antitrust Division of the Department of Justice—Agency designed to prevent monopolistic business activities, thereby encouraging competition. The Department of Justice may examine proposed bank mergers for potential antitrust violations.

Securities and Exchange Commission—Independent federal regulatory agency created by the Securities and Exchange Act of 1934 to protect investors; maintain fair, orderly, and efficient markets; and facilitate capital formation.

Federal Trade Commission—Federal agency that enforces various laws that restrict anti-competitive practices and protect consumers.

Consumer Financial Protection Bureau—This was established by Congress in the Dodd-Frank Act of 2010 to protect consumers by carrying out Federal consumer financial laws.

Basel Committee on Banking Supervision—This international body created by the governors of the Central Banks of the Group of 10 nations does not have direct regulatory authority over U.S. banks. However, it formulates guidelines that U.S. regulators often follow in an attempt to enhance the consistency of bank regulation.